THE
LARGE
TYPE
COOK
BOOK

Other Cookbooks by Avanelle S. Day
Herb and Spice Sampler Cookbook
The Spice Cookbook
(*co-author with Lillie Stuckey*)

AVANELLE DAY learned to cook in childhood. She earned a bachelor's degree in Home Economics at Women's College of Georgia, and later a master's degree at Columbia University. After several years of teaching in junior and senior high schools and in cafeteria management, Mrs. Day has spent twenty years in recipe research, especially in spice cookery. During this time she has tested and perfected thousands of recipes, and from this rich experience she has written this book to make cooking easier and more enjoyable for its readers.

THE LARGE TYPE COOK BOOK

Avanelle S. Day

DAVID WHITE

NEW YORK

FIRST EDITION

Published in the United States of America by
David White, Inc., 60 East 55th Street,
New York, N. Y. 10022

Library of Congress Catalog Card Number: 68-29371

Manufactured in the United States of America

CONTENTS

THE
LARGE
TYPE
COOK
BOOK

INTRODUCTION

This book has been written to help the housewife with aging or ailing eyes to prepare meals with the minimum effort compatible with good results.

Its large type will appeal both to those who have difficulty reading fine print even while wearing glasses, and to those who use glasses for reading but prefer not to wear them while cooking. There are also features which should have an equal appeal to cooks with normal eyesight.

With a few exceptions, the recipes are short, with as few steps of preparation as are possible without detracting from the quality of the finished product. A special effort was made to include recipes for dishes that can be prepared in one operation. Those include dishes in which the ingredients are placed in a casserole, cooked in the oven, and served at the table from the casserole. Also, use is made of many of the convenience foods found on the shelves of supermarkets. These, too, reduce the time and effort of food preparation.

These recipes are not especially bizarre but include all categories necessary to prepare flavorful and nutritious family meals as well as more glamorous ones for guests. Special recipes have been provided for those on weight-reducing, sugar-restricted, or low-salt diets.

When the name of a dish is capitalized in the text, a recipe for that dish will be found elsewhere in the book.

The menu suggestions at the end of various main-dish recipes should be found useful.

—Avanelle Day

APPETIZERS

Appetizers should be prepared with two things in mind: that they be eye-catchers and appetite-whetters. This rule applies as much to the simplest bowl of soup or glass of tomato juice as it does to an elaborate seafood or fruit combination, or even to a fancy canapé or hors d'oeuvre.

BROILED GINGERED GRAPEFRUIT

1 large grapefruit, cut in cross-wise halves

1 teaspoon finely chopped preserved ginger

2 teaspoons syrup from preserved ginger

1. Remove seeds from grapefruit halves. Separate the sections from the membrane. Remove the center core.
2. Put 1/2 teaspoon finely chopped preserved ginger in the center of each half.
3. Sprinkle 1 teaspoon ginger syrup over each half.
4. Place in a preheated slow broiler until grapefruit is hot and the top is lightly flecked with brown.

5. Serve for the first course for breakfast or brunch, or as a dessert.

Broiler temperature: 325°F. (slow).

Broiling time: 5 to 6 minutes.

Yield: 2 servings.

BLUE-CHEESE-STUFFED CELERY

1/4 cup crumbled blue cheese
3-ounce package cream cheese
dash cayenne

6 ribs celery, 8 to 9 inches long, washed and dried
paprika or chopped parsley

1. Combine the first 3 ingredients and mix well.
2. With a spatula or the tip of a teaspoon, stuff cheese mixture into the ribs of celery.
3. Cut the ribs into pieces 2-1/2 to 3 inches long.
4. Sprinkle with paprika or chopped parsley.

Yield: 12 3-inch pieces.

HOT BLUE CHEESE CANAPÉS

1 package (4 ounces) cream cheese
2 tablespoons crumbled blue cheese
1 tablespoon catsup
1-3/4 teaspoons chili powder

1/4 teaspoon paprika
1/16 teaspoon garlic powder

10 slices firm-textured bread, toasted on one side, crusts removed
snipped parsley

1. Combine the first 6 ingredients. Mix well.
2. Spread mixture on untoasted side of the bread.

3. Cut each slice into 3 finger-length strips and arrange slices on cooky sheets.
4. Broil in the oven broiler until the spread is bubbly and well flecked with brown.
5. Garnish with snipped parsley. Serve hot.

Oven broiler temperature: 550°F. (broil).

Broiling time: 3 to 4 minutes.

Yield: Approximately 2-1/2 dozen canapés.

CHEESE AND HAM BALLS

1 cup (1/4 pound) grated Swiss cheese
1 cup ground cooked ham
1 egg yolk, uncooked
1 teaspoon Dijon-type pre-

pared mustard or mustard to taste
salt to taste
snipped parsley or chives

1. Combine the first 5 ingredients.
2. Shape the mixture into 3/4-inch balls.
3. Roll balls in snipped parsley or snipped chives.
4. Chill. Serve with toothpicks.

Yield: Approximately 2 dozen balls.

CHILI PINWHEEL CANAPÉS

3-ounce package cream cheese
2 teaspoons finely snipped parsley
2 teaspoons milk
1/2 teaspoon chili powder or chili powder to taste

dash garlic salt or onion salt
4 slices spiced ham or pressed ham
30 unsweetened crackers, or 30 rounds toasted bread or fried bread

1. Combine the first 5 ingredients.
2. Place 2 slices ham, with ends overlapping 1/2 inch, on a flat surface.
3. Spread half the cream-cheese mixture over the ham and roll it up as for a jelly roll.
4. Repeat the procedure, using the remaining ingredients.
5. Wrap rolls in clear plastic or foil and chill 3 to 4 hours or overnight.
6. Cut rolls into slices 1/8 inch thick and serve the slices on unsweetened crackers, or on rounds of toasted bread or fried bread.

Yield: 30 servings.

CURRIED PINWHEEL CANAPÉS

In the recipe for Chili Pinwheel Canapés, replace chili powder with 3/4 teaspoon curry powder or curry powder to taste. Proceed according to directions in the recipe.
Yield: 30 canapés.

CHICKEN LIVER AND BACON HORS D'OEUVRE

chicken livers
simmering water
salt

bacon slices, cut in half (allow 1/2 slice for each hors d'oeuvre)

1. Cook chicken livers, uncovered, in simmering salted water to cover (1/2 teaspoon salt to 2 cups water) until livers are tender, 15 to 20 minutes.
2. Cook bacon slices until half-done.

3. Remove livers and drain them well.
4. Cut livers in half if they are large; leave them whole if they are small.
5. Wrap each liver or half liver in 1/2 slice of partially cooked bacon.
6. Fasten ends of bacon to the liver with toothpicks. Place hors d'oeuvres on a rack in a shallow baking pan.
7. Broil in a preheated broiler until bacon is brown and crisp, turning occasionally.
8. Serve hot with the toothpicks still in place.

Broiler temperature: 550°F. (broiling temperature).

Broiling time: 5 to 7 minutes.

Allow 3 hors d'oeuvres per person.

EASY-TO-MAKE MEAT TURNOVERS

These may be made the day before and reheated just before serving. Frozen pastry, pastry made from a mix, or homemade pastry may be used instead of the ready-to-cook biscuits.

1/2 teaspoon powdered mustard

1/4 cup water

1 tablespoon flour

2 tablespoons butter or margarine, melted

1/2 pound (1 cup) ground chuck

1/2 teaspoon instant minced onion, or 1-1/2 teaspoons chopped raw onion

1/2 teaspoon salt or salt to taste

1/2 teaspoon to 3/4 teaspoon chili powder

2 packages (6 biscuits each) ready-to-cook biscuits

1. Mix mustard with water and set the mixture aside.
2. Blend flour with 1 tablespoon of the melted butter or margarine in a skillet.
3. Stir in mustard water and the next 4 ingredients.
4. Cook over medium heat, stirring, 5 to 8 minutes.
5. Split each ready-to-cook biscuit in half, using the fingers.
6. Roll each half biscuit in a circle 1/16 inch thick.
7. Put 1 teaspoon of the filling slightly off center on each.
8. Fold the dough over the filling and press the edges together with the index finger; crimp edges with a fork, dipping the fork in flour frequently to prevent sticking.
9. Place turnovers on a greased baking sheet, and brush tops with the remaining 1 tablespoon butter or margarine.
10. Bake in a preheated hot oven until turnovers have browned.
11. Serve hot as an accompaniment to cocktails, tea, or coffee.

Oven temperature: 400°F. (hot).

Baking time: 10 to 12 minutes.

Yield: 2 dozen turnovers.

VARIATIONS

OYSTER TURNOVERS

24 soup oysters, cut in half
1/8 teaspoon ground black pepper
1/4 teaspoon salt

1/4 teaspoon celery seed

2 packages (6 biscuits each) ready-to-cook biscuits

1. Drain oysters well, and mix them with the next three ingredients.
2. Roll biscuits as in recipe for Meat Turnovers.
3. Place half an oyster, slightly off center, on each.
4. Seal edges and bake as in to the recipe for Meat Turnovers.

Yield: 2 dozen turnovers.

CURRIED CHICKEN-LIVER TURNOVERS

3/4 cup raw chicken livers
simmering water
salt

1/8 teaspoon ground black pepper
1 teaspoon curry powder

2 hard-cooked eggs, chopped fine

3 to 4 tablespoons heavy cream

1/4 teaspoon instant minced onion or 1 teaspoon chopped raw onion

2 packages (6 biscuits each) ready-to-cook biscuits

1. Poach chicken livers in enough salted simmering water (1/4 teaspoon salt to 1 cup water) to cover until they lose their pink color.
2. Drain chicken livers well, put them in a chopping bowl, and chop very fine.
3. Add the next 4 ingredients and mix well.
4. Stir in 1/4 teaspoon salt and enough cream to moisten the mixture.
5. Put the mixture through a coarse sieve.
6. Roll biscuits, fill, seal edges, and bake according to the recipe for Meat Turnovers.

Yield: 2 dozen turnovers.

PIQUANT CHEESE BALLS

1 cup (1/4 pound) finely shredded sharp Cheddar cheese

2 ounces blue cheese

3-ounce package cream cheese

1/16 teaspoon onion powder or 1/4 teaspoon grated raw onion

dash garlic powder or a dash crushed fresh garlic

1/4 to 1/2 teaspoon red hot sauce or tabasco sauce

snipped parsley, Toasted Sesame Seeds, or imported paprika

1. Combine the first 6 ingredients and chill until the mixture is stiff enough to handle, about 2 hours.
2. Shape the mixture into 1/2-inch balls.
3. Roll the balls in snipped parsley, Toasted Sesame Seeds, or paprika.
4. Serve as a cocktail accompaniment or as a garnish for vegetable, seafood, meat, or poultry salads.

Yield: Approximately 3-1/2 dozen balls.

MELON WITH ITALIAN PROSCIUTTO

1 large honeydew, casaba, or Spanish melon

1/4 pound thinly sliced prosciutto (Italian ham)

6 lemon wedges or lime wedges

1. Cut melon in half, remove seeds, and cut off the rind.
2. Cut each half melon into 6 wedges. Put 2 wedges on a salad plate or dessert plate for each serving.
3. Cut prosciutto into strips about 1 inch wide and drape a

strip over each melon wedge, or if desired, roll up the prosciutto strips and place 2 rolls on each plate beside the melon wedges.

4. Garnish with a lemon or lime wedge.
5. Serve as an appetizer. Eat with a knife and fork.

Yield: 6 servings.

MELON ANTIPASTO

Wrap bite-size pieces or wedges of cantaloupe, casaba melon, honeydew melon, or Spanish melon in prosciutto (Italian ham) or in slices of dried chipped beef. Serve on toothpicks with black olives or green olives. Allow 2 to 3 per person.

SHRIMP-STUFFED MUSHROOMS

15 to 20 small raw mushrooms, 3/4 to 1 inch diameter

2 tablespoons grated sharp Cheddar cheese

2 tablespoons fine dry breadcrumbs

1/4 teaspoon instant minced onion or 1 teaspoon grated raw onion

3/4 teaspoon salt or salt to taste

1/2 cup minced canned shrimp or cooked fresh shrimp

parsley

1. Wash mushrooms and remove stems.
2. Reserve mushroom caps whole, but chop the stems very fine.
3. Mix the chopped stems with the next 5 ingredients.

4. Fill mushroom caps with shrimp stuffing, and arrange them on a baking sheet.
5. Broil in a preheated broiler oven (oven control set to broil) until mushrooms have browned.

Oven temperature: Set to broil, 550°F.

Broiling time: 5 to 10 minutes.

Yield: 15 to 20 stuffed mushroom caps.

HAM-STUFFED MUSHROOMS

In the recipe for Shrimp-Stuffed Mushrooms, replace the minced shrimp with 1/2 cup ground cooked ham. If ham is salty, reduce salt to 1/2 teaspoon or salt to taste.

CANAPÉ SPREADS

ANCHOVY AND CREAM CHEESE SPREAD

1-1/2 teaspoons anchovy paste
3-ounce package cream cheese
assorted fancy shapes fried bread, unsweetened crackers, or 1/8-inch slices unpeeled cucumber
parsley or paprika

1. Blend anchovy paste with cream cheese.
2. Spread cheese mixture over the fried bread, unsweetened crackers, or cucumber slices. Garnish with parsley or paprika.
3. If desired, put the spread in a small bowl, place it in the

center of a round tray, and surround it with the fried bread, crackers, or cucumber slices.

Yield: 1/3 cup or sufficient spread for about 25 small canapés.

BACON-CHEESE SPREAD

Use this tasty spread for sandwiches, unsweetened crackers, or for stuffing celery.

2 cups (1/2 pound) grated sharp Cheddar cheese
6 tablespoons milk or light cream
1/2 teaspoon salt

1/2 teaspoon ground ginger
1/8 teaspoon ground black pepper
_____
6 slices crisp bacon, crumbled

1. Combine the first 5 ingredients and mix well.
2. Add crumbled bacon, and mix until well blended.
Yield: 2 cups.

CURRIED-EGG SPREAD

3 large hard-cooked eggs, chopped very fine
2 tablespoons finely chopped celery
2 tablespoons mayonnaise
1/2 teaspoon salt
1/16 teaspoon ground black pepper

1 teaspoon curry powder
_____
assorted fancy shapes of fried bread, unsweetened crackers, or unpeeled cucumber slices
pimiento, cut in short narrow strips, or parsley

1. Combine the first 6 ingredients and mix well.
2. Spread the egg mixture over the fried bread, unsweetened crackers, or cucumber slices.
3. Garnish with pimiento cut into narrow, short strips, or with parsley.

Yield: 1 cup or sufficient spread for about 50 canapés.

DEVILED-HAM SPREAD

2 tablespoons finely chopped celery

2 teaspoons pickle relish or finely chopped gherkins

4-1/2-ounce can deviled ham

assorted shapes of fried bread, unsweetened crackers or unpeeled cucumber slices

chopped parsley or watercress leaves

1. Combine the first 3 ingredients and mix well.
2. Spread the mixture over fried bread, unsweetened crackers, or unpeeled cucumber slices.
3. Roll or dip the edges of the canapés in chopped parsley, or put 3 small watercress leaves in the center of each.

Yield: 1/2 cup or sufficient spread for about 25 canapés.

DIPS

CHEESE AND ONION DIP

3-ounce package cream cheese

1/3 cup crumbled blue cheese

1/2 cup mayonnaise

1/4 teaspoon salt or more

2 teaspoons instant minced onion

dash garlic powder

dash ground black pepper

1. Put the cheeses in a 1-quart mixing bowl and mix well.
2. Add the remaining ingredients and stir until all the ingredients are blended.
3. Serve as a dip for fresh vegetable sticks, potato chips, or crackers.

Yield: 1 cup.

AVOCADO AND CREAM CHEESE DIP

1 medium-sized ripe avocado
1 teaspoon lemon juice

3-ounce package cream cheese
2 teaspoons finely chopped parsley

3/4 teaspoon grated onion
1/16 teaspoon garlic juice or instant minced garlic
dash cayenne
----
paprika

1. Cut the avocado in half and remove the seed and the avocado meat, keeping the half shells intact to use as bowls for serving the dip.
2. Dice the avocado meat into the lemon juice to prevent discoloration.
3. Mash the avocado with a fork.
4. Add the next 5 ingredients and mix well.
5. Pile the dip lightly into the avocado shells and sprinkle with paprika.
6. Place the filled avocado shells in the center of a serving plate or tray, and arrange raw vegetable sticks, potato chips, cooked shrimp, or unsweetened crackers around them.
7. Serve as an accompaniment to vegetable juices or cocktails.

Yield: 1-1/3 cups.

GUACAMOLE

1 medium-sized ripe avocado
2 teaspoons lemon juice

1/3 cup finely chopped peeled tomato
1 tablespoon finely chopped onion
1/8 teaspoon garlic juice or a

dash of instant minced garlic
1/4 teaspoon salt or salt to taste
ground black pepper to taste
dash cayenne

1. Peel the avocado and dice it into the lemon juice. This prevents the avocado from discoloring.
2. Mash the mixture well with a fork.
3. Stir in all the remaining ingredients.
4. Serve as a dip for an appetizer or as a cocktail accompaniment.
5. Guacamole may be made 2 to 3 hours before serving without discoloring if the avocado seed is placed on the top of the mixture, and the bowl is covered and placed in the refrigerator.

Makes 3/4 cup.

HUNGARIAN CARAWAY-SEED DIP

8-ounce package cream cheese, softened
1/4 cup (1/2 stick) unsalted butter, softened
1-1/4 teaspoons salt

2 tablespoons imported Hungarian paprika
1 teaspoon powdered mustard soaked in 1 teaspoon water
4 teaspoons caraway seed

1. Combine all ingredients in a 1-quart mixing bowl and blend well.
2. Refrigerate several hours or overnight.
3. Remove the dip from the refrigerator about 1 hour before serving so it will soften.
4. Serve as a dip for vegetable sticks, potato chips, and unsweetened crackers.

Yield: 1-1/4 cups.

TOMATO-CLAM DIP

3-ounce package cream cheese

2 tablespoons finely chopped, peeled fresh tomato

2 tablespoons canned minced clams

1 tablespoon clam juice

1-1/2 tablespoons minced parsley

3/4 teaspoon salt or salt to taste

1/16 teaspoon ground black pepper

1/16 teaspoon minced fresh garlic or a dash garlic powder

1. Put the cream cheese in a small mixing bowl and stir until it is soft.
2. Add all the remaining ingredients and mix well.
3. Serve as a dip for vegetable sticks, potato chips, corn chips, or crackers.

Yield: 1 cup.

BEVERAGES

CRANBERRY JUICE

2 cups raw cranberries, washed
3 whole cloves
2 cups water

2/3 cup sugar
1/4 cup orange juice
1 tablespoon lemon juice
dash salt

1. Put the first 3 ingredients in a 1-1/2-quart saucepan. Cook, covered, until cranberry skins pop, 8 to 10 minutes.
2. Remove cranberries from heat, cool slightly, and strain.
3. Add remaining ingredients to the juice; mix well. Chill.
4. Serve in fruit juice glasses over a small amount of cracked ice, if desired.

Yield: Approximately 3-1/2 cups.

CUCUMBER LEMONADE

An old-fashioned lemonade, subtly flavored with cucumbers, that was served in the south to afternoon guests by our mothers and grandmothers.

1 cup sugar

1 cup water

1 cup lemon juice

all lemon rinds

4 cups water

ice cubes

12 cucumber slices

1. Put the sugar, water, and 1/4 cup of the lemon juice in a 1-quart saucepan. Mix well, bring to boiling point, and boil 1 to 2 minutes.
2. Add all the lemon rinds to the hot syrup, and let them steep 2 to 3 minutes. (If rinds are left in the syrup too long, syrup will be bitter.)
3. Remove rinds from syrup and discard them.
4. Add remaining lemon juice and the water to syrup. Cool.
5. Place 2 to 3 ice cubes and 2 cucumber slices in each tall glass, and fill with the lemonade.

Yield: 6 tall glasses.

WATERMELON LEMONADE

1/2 cup sugar

1 cup water

3/4 cup lemon juice

6 cups diced ripe watermelon

fresh mint

1. Mix sugar, water, and 1 tablespoon of the lemon juice in a saucepan.
2. Bring the mixture to boiling point and boil 1/2 minute, stirring constantly. Remove from heat and cool.
3. Put watermelon through a fine sieve and add the juice to the cooled sugar syrup. (There should be 3 cups watermelon juice.)

4. Stir in the remaining lemon juice.

5. Serve in tall glasses over ice cubes. Garnish with fresh mint. Yield: 6 servings.

FRUIT PUNCH

1/2 cup sugar
1 cup water
_____
1/2 cup lemon juice
1-1/2 cups apricot juice or peach juice

2 cups canned or frozen grapefruit juice
2-1/2 cups canned pineapple juice
_____
orange slices and lemon slices

1. Combine sugar and water in a saucepan, bring to boiling point, and boil 1 minute.
2. Cool the syrup, and stir in the next 4 ingredients.
3. Put ice in a punch bowl and pour in punch.
4. Float orange and lemon slices over the surface.
5. Serve in punch cups.
Yield: 2 quarts or 16 servings.

CHAMPAGNE PUNCH

Perfect to serve at an anniversary party or at other very special celebrations.

3 cups sugar
2 cups hot water
1-1/4 cups lemon juice
1 cup lime juice
1 quart ice water

1 bottle (24 ounces) sauterne or Rhine wine, chilled
1 bottle (24 ounces) champagne, chilled

1. Mix sugar, hot water, and 1/4 cup of the lemon juice in a 2-quart saucepan.
2. Bring the mixture to boiling point, stirring, and simmer 3 to 4 minutes.
3. Remove the syrup from the heat and cool.
4. Just before serving, add the remaining 1 cup lemon juice, lime juice, and ice water.
5. Pour the mixture into a punch bowl. Then stir in the wine. Last add the champagne. Serve in punch cups.

Yield: Approximately 4 quarts.

HOT SPICED PUNCH

1/2 cup sugar
1 cup water
3 sticks cinnamon, each 2 inches long
4 ginger roots, each 1 inch long
1/2 teaspoon whole allspice
1/2 teaspoon whole cloves

1/2 cup lemon juice
2-1/2 cups canned pineapple juice
2 cups apple juice
2 cups grapefruit juice, canned or frozen

lemon slices studded with whole cloves for garnish

1. Put the first 6 ingredients in a small saucepan, mix well, bring to boiling point, and boil 3 minutes.
2. Pour syrup through a sieve to strain out spices.
3. Combine syrup and all the fruit juices in a 3-quart saucepan. Heat only until the punch is hot.
4. Serve hot in mugs with a slice of lemon studded with a whole clove floating over the top. Or if desired pour into a

punch bowl and float lemon slices studded with cloves over the surface. Serve in punch cups.

Yield: Approximately 2 quarts or 16 servings.

SPICED COCOA

1/3 cup sugar
1/4 cup unsweetened cocoa
1/16 teaspoon salt
3/4 cup water
6 whole cloves

3 cups milk
1/2 cup light cream

6 cinnamon sticks 3 to 4 inches
  long

1. Put the first 5 ingredients in a 1-1/2-quart saucepan.
2. Mix well and boil gently for 3 minutes.
3. Add milk and light cream. Heat only until hot, stirring frequently to prevent a scum from forming over the surface.
4. Serve hot in mugs with a stick of cinnamon in each to use as a muddler.

Yield: 1 generous quart or 6 servings.

BREADS

Few foods add as much to a meal as does homemade bread, whether it be a quick bread served hot from the oven, or a yeast bread with its tantalizing aroma to whet the appetite. The recipes in this chapter include conventional methods of making breads, and also methods involving the use of such convenience foods as dough mixes and refrigerated or frozen packaged unbaked breads.

ANGEL BISCUIT

This dough will keep for a week in the refrigerator, if kept covered. Bake the biscuits as you need them.

6 cups sifted self-rising flour
1/3 cup sugar
1 teaspoon soda
1 envelope active dry yeast
1 cup shortening
2 cups buttermilk

1. Sift 5-3/4 cups of the flour, sugar, and soda into a 2-1/2-quart mixing bowl.
2. Add yeast and mix well.

3. Add shortening to flour mixture, and cut it in with a pastry blender or with fingers until mixture resembles crumbs.

4. Stir in buttermilk.

5. Turn dough onto a flat surface, and knead in the remaining 1/4 cup flour.

6. Roll dough to 1/4 inch thickness. Shape biscuits with a 2-1/2-inch cooky cutter dipped in flour to prevent it from sticking to the dough.

7. Arrange biscuits on an ungreased cooky sheet. Bake in a preheated very hot oven until biscuits have browned. Serve hot.

Oven temperature: 450°F. (very hot).

Baking time: 12 to 15 minutes.

Yield: Approximately 5-1/2 dozen biscuits.

SOUTHERN BISCUIT

2 cups sifted all-purpose flour
3 teaspoons double-acting baking powder

1 teaspoon salt

1/4 cup shortening
about 3/4 cup milk

1. Sift the first 3 ingredients together into a 2-quart mixing bowl.

2. Add shortening and with a pastry blender or 2 knives cut it in until mixture resembles coarse crumbs.

3. Gradually stir in enough milk to form a dough that is soft enough to knead, but not sticky.

4. Knead the dough about 20 seconds on a lightly floured flat surface.

5. With a lightly floured rolling pin, roll the dough to about 1/3 inch thickness.
6. Cut the dough into biscuits with a 2-inch biscuit cutter, cutting edge dipped in flour.
7. Place biscuits 1/2 inch apart on ungreased cooky sheets.
8. Bake in a preheated very hot oven until biscuits have browned.

Oven temperature: 450°F. (very hot).
Baking time: 12 to 15 minutes.
Yield: About 18 biscuits.

CHEESE PINWHEELS

2 cups sifted all-purpose flour
3/4 teaspoon salt
3 teaspoons double-acting baking powder

1/4 cup shortening

1 cup (1/4 pound) grated sharp Cheddar cheese
2/3 to 3/4 cup milk
3 tablespoons butter or margarine, softened

1. Sift the first 3 ingredients together into a 1-1/2-quart mixing bowl.
2. Add the shortening and 1/2 cup of the cheese. With a pastry blender or two knives, cut in the cheese and shortening until the mixture resembles coarse cornmeal.
3. Stir in enough milk to form a soft dough that can be rolled.
4. Knead dough about 20 seconds on a lightly floured flat surface. Roll it 1/4 inch thick into a 16 x 7-inch rectangle.
5. Spread surface of dough with softened butter or margarine and sprinkle with the remaining 1/2 cup grated cheese.

6. Roll up dough tightly, as for jelly roll, beginning at the wide side.

7. Cut the roll in slices 3/4 inch thick and place the slices on lightly greased cooky sheets.

8. Bake in a very hot oven until golden brown. Serve hot.

Oven temperature: 450°F. (very hot).

Baking time: 12 to 15 minutes.

Yield: About 16 pinwheels.

BUTTERSCOTCH PINWHEELS

1 recipe Southern Biscuit dough

6 tablespoons butter or margarine, softened

1/3 cup light or dark brown sugar, firmly packed

1. Make Southern Biscuit dough and roll it into a 16 x 7 x 1/4-inch rectangle on a lightly floured flat surface.

2. Combine softened butter or margarine and brown sugar.

3. Spread the mixture over the rolled dough.

4. Roll the dough up tightly in jelly-roll fashion, beginning at the long side (16-inch side).

5. Cut the roll into slices about 3/4 inch thick.

6. Place the slices in greased muffin cups or on greased cooky sheets.

7. Bake in a preheated hot oven until pinwheels have browned.

8. Serve hot.

Oven temperature: 400°F. (hot).

Baking time: 15 to 20 minutes.

Yield: Approximately 16 pinwheels.

VARIATIONS

CINNAMON PINWHEELS

1. Spread rolled rectangle of Southern Biscuit dough with 4 tablespoons (1/2 stick) softened butter or margarine.
2. Mix 1/3 cup granulated sugar with 1 teaspoon ground cinnamon and sprinkle mixture over buttered dough.
3. If desired, sprinkle with dried currants or raisins.
4. Roll up dough as for jelly roll, cut into slices, and bake according to directions in recipe for Butterscotch Pinwheels.

Yield: Approximately 16 pinwheels.

DEVILED-HAM PINWHEELS

1. Soak 1/4 teaspoon powdered mustard in 1/2 teaspoon water and mix with 3-ounce can of deviled ham.
2. Spread ham mixture over the rolled rectangle of Southern Biscuit dough.
3. Roll up dough as for jelly roll, cut into slices, and bake according to directions in recipe for Butterscotch Pinwheels.

Yield: Approximately 16 pinwheels.

ORANGE TEA PINWHEELS

1. Brush a rectangle of Southern Biscuit Dough with 3 tablespoons softened butter or margarine.
2. Sprinkle the dough with 1/4 cup granulated sugar and 1/2 cup finely chopped candied orange peel.
3. Roll up dough as for jelly roll, cut into slices, and bake

according to directions in recipe for Butterscotch Pinwheels. If desired, brush Orange Glaze over the tops of cooled rolls.

Yield: Approximately 16 pinwheels.

MARMALADE PINWHEELS

1. Melt 3 tablespoons butter or margarine; brush it over the surface of a rectangle of Southern Biscuit dough.
2. Then spread dough with 1/2 cup thick orange, peach, or apricot marmalade or jam.
3. Roll up dough as for jelly roll, cut into slices, and bake according to directions in recipe for Butterscotch Pinwheels. If desired, before baking pinwheels brush the tops with melted butter or margarine.

Yield: Approximately 16 pinwheels.

CORNBREAD

1 cup sifted all-purpose flour
1/2 teaspoon soda
3/4 teaspoon salt
2 teaspoons double-acting baking powder

1 large egg, unbeaten
1 cup sour milk or buttermilk
1/3 cup water
1/4 cup shortening or bacon drippings, melted

1 cup cornmeal

1. Sift the first 4 ingredients together into a 2-quart mixing bowl.
2. Add the cornmeal to the flour mixture and mix well.

3. Add all the remaining ingredients and mix until they are well blended.
4. Pour the batter into a hot, well-greased 8 x 8 x 2-inch baking pan.
5. Bake until cornbread is well browned. Serve hot.

Oven temperature: 450°F. (very hot).

Baking time: approximately 30 minutes.

Yield: 9 squares, 2-1/2 inches each.

BANANA PEANUT-BUTTER BREAD

This bread improves with age. Make it 2 to 3 days before serving for best flavor.

1-3/4 cups sifted all-purpose flour

1-3/4 teaspoons double-acting baking powder

1/2 teaspoon soda

1/2 teaspoon salt

1-1/2 teaspoons vanilla extract

3/4 cup crunchy peanut butter

3/4 cup sugar

2 large eggs

1 cup mashed bananas (2 to 3 bananas)

3 tablespoons milk

1. Sift flour with baking powder and set aside.
2. Put next 4 ingredients in a mixing bowl; mix well.
3. Blend in 1/4 cup sugar. Beat in 1 of the eggs.
4. Gradually add remaining 1/2 cup sugar and egg.
5. Add flour mixture alternately with mashed banana and milk, mixing only until ingredients are blended.
7. Turn the batter into a well-greased, lightly floured 9 x 5 x 3-inch loaf pan.

8. Bake in a preheated moderate oven until a cake tester inserted in the center comes out clean.
9. Turn the bread out onto a wire rack to cool.
10. Wrap bread in foil and store it in a plastic bag or in a bread box. Serve with butter or cream cheese.

Oven temperature: 350°F. (moderate).
Baking time: 50 to 60 minutes.
Yield: 1 loaf, 9 x 5 x 3 inches.

CINNAMON YEAST BREAD

13-3/4-ounce package yeast-roll mix
3 tablespoons butter or margarine, melted
1/4 cup sugar
3/4 teaspoon ground cinnamon

1. Prepare yeast dough according to directions on the package and let it rise once in a warm place (80 to 85°F.) until the dough has doubled in size.
2. Punch down the dough and roll it on a lightly floured flat surface into a 14 x 9 x 1/2-inch rectangle.
3. Brush the dough with melted butter or margarine.
4. Combine sugar and cinnamon and sprinkle the mixture over the dough.
5. Roll up the dough in jelly-roll fashion, starting from the long side.
6. Place the roll in a greased 9 x 5 x 3-inch loaf pan.
7. Cover and let rise in a warm place (80 to 85°F.) until the loaf has doubled in size.

8. Bake in a preheated moderate oven until browned.
Oven temperature: 375°F. (moderate).
Baking time: 40 minutes.
Yield: One 9-inch loaf.

DATE AND NUT LOAF

1/2 cup diced dried dates

1-1/2 cups boiling water

3 tablespoons butter or margarine

1 cup sugar

1 teaspoon salt

1 teaspoon vanilla extract

1 large egg, well beaten

2-2/3 cups sifted all-purpose flour

1 teaspoon cream of tartar

1 teaspoon soda

1 cup chopped pecans

1. Put the first 6 ingredients in a 2-quart mixing bowl, mix well, and cool.
2. Stir in the beaten egg.
3. Sift the flour again with the cream of tartar and soda and gradually add to the date and water mixture. Mix well.
4. Stir in the pecans.
5. Turn the batter into a well-greased, lightly floured 9 x 5 x 3-inch loaf pan.
6. Bake until a toothpick or cake tester inserted in the center comes out clean. Turn loaf out onto a wire rack to cool.

Oven temperature: 350°F. (moderate).
Baking time: 60 to 70 minutes.
Yield: One 9 x 5 x 3-inch loaf.

GARLIC FRENCH BREAD

1 loaf French bread
1/2 cup (1 stick) butter or margarine, softened

1/4 teaspoon instant minced garlic or 1 clove garlic, crushed

1. Make diagonal cuts in the French bread at 1-inch intervals. Do not cut through the bottom.
2. Combine butter or margarine and garlic.
3. Spread the butter mixture between the bread slices.
4. Place the bread on a cooky sheet and sprinkle the top with a few drops of water.
5. Bake in a preheated moderate oven until hot.

Oven temperature: 350°F. (moderate).
Baking time: about 10 to 12 minutes.
Yield: Approximately 12 servings.

ONION FRENCH BREAD

In the recipe for Garlic French Bread, replace the garlic with 1/2 teaspoon instant minced onion. Continue according to the recipe.
Yield: Approximately 12 servings.

CHRISTMAS COFFEE RING

Make this coffee ring the day before Christmas. Then on Christmas morning just heat it a few mintues in the oven, and serve for breakfast.

1 package (13-3/4 ounces) yeast-roll mix

3 tablespoons butter or margarine, melted
_____

1/3 cup sugar

1/4 teaspoon ground cardamon

1 teaspoon grated lemon rind
_____

1/2 cup mixed glacéed fruit or raisins, diced

1. Prepare yeast dough according to directions on package and let it rise one time in a warm place (80 to 85°F.) until the dough has doubled in size.
2. Roll dough on a lightly floured flat surface into an 18 x 8 x 1/4-inch rectangle.
3. Brush the dough with melted butter or margarine.
4. Combine the next 3 ingredients and sprinkle the mixture over the dough to within 1/2 inch of the edges.
5. Sprinkle with diced glacéed fruit or raisins.
6. Roll up the dough in jelly-roll fashion, starting at the long side (18-inch side) of the dough.
7. Place the roll on a greased baking sheet and form it into a ring. Pinch the ends together.
8. Cover the ring with a damp cloth and let it rise in a warm place until it has doubled in size.
9. Bake in a preheated moderate oven until browned.
10. If desired, mix about 1 teaspoon water with 1/4 cup sifted confectioners' sugar, brush over top of ring, and sprinkle with additional glacéed fruit or raisins.

Oven temperature: 375°F. (moderate).

Baking time: 30 minutes.

Yield: One 9-inch coffee ring or 6 servings.

DELICIOUS BRAN MUFFINS

1-1/4 cups sifted all-purpose flour

1 teaspoon double-acting baking powder

1/2 teaspoon salt

1/4 teaspoon soda

3/4 cup all-bran

1/4 cup sugar

1/4 cup shortening

1/4 cup honey

1 egg, beaten slightly

1/2 cup milk

1. Sift the first 4 ingredients together into a 2-quart mixing bowl, stir in all-bran, and set aside.
2. Blend sugar with shortening. Add honey and mix well.
3. Beat in egg. Add dry ingredients alternately with milk.
4. Fill paper-lined 2-1/2-inch muffin cups or well-greased muffin cups three-fourths full with the batter.
5. Bake in a preheated hot oven until muffins have browned.

Oven temperature: 400°F. (hot).

Baking time: 15 minutes.

Yield: 12 muffins.

VARIATIONS

RAISIN-BRAN MUFFINS

Stir 1/2 cup seedless raisins into the Delicious Bran Muffin batter.

DATE-BRAN MUFFINS

Stir 1/2 cup chopped pitted dried dates into the Delicious Bran Muffin batter.

ONION CORN MUFFINS

12-ounce package corn muffin mix

1-1/2 tablespoons instant minced onion

egg (see package directions)

milk (see package directions)

1. Empty contents of package of mix into a mixing bowl.
2. Add instant minced onion and mix well.
3. Add egg or eggs, if specified in package directions.
4. Stir in amount of milk specified in package directions.
5. Spoon the mixture into paper-lined muffin cups or into well-greased muffin cups, filling them half full.
6. Bake in a preheated hot oven until golden brown.

Oven temperature: 400°F. (hot).

Baking time: 15 to 20 minutes.

Yield: 12 muffins.

ALL-PURPOSE ROLLS

about 4-1/2 cups sifted all-purpose flour

1/3 cup sugar
2 teaspoons salt
2 envelopes active dry yeast

1-1/4 cups milk

1/2 cup (1 stick) butter or margarine, softened

1 large egg

1. Combine 2 cups of the flour with the next 3 ingredients in a 2-1/2-quart mixing bowl.
2. Heat milk with butter, only until milk is hot (not boiling). (It is unnecessary to melt the butter.)

3. Gradually stir milk and butter into the flour mixture.
4. Beat in egg. Continue beating until the batter falls in a sheet from the spoon.
5. Stir in 2 more cups of the flour. Turn dough onto a flat surface and knead in the remaining 1/2 cup flour or enough flour to make the dough stiff enough to be handled without sticking to the hands.
6. Knead dough until it is elastic and satiny.
7. Place dough in a greased bowl, turning to bring the greased surface to the top.
8. Cover the bowl, and let the dough rise until it has doubled in size, 1 to 1-1/2 hours.
9. Punch down dough. Shape into a ball, cover, and let rest 10 minutes.
10. Shape dough into rolls desired (see How to Shape Rolls), and place them on greased cooky sheets.
11. Cover and let rolls rise until they have doubled in size, 40 to 50 minutes.
12. Bake rolls in a preheated hot oven until browned.

Oven temperature: 400°F. (hot).

Baking time: 12 to 15 minutes.

Yield: 2-1/2 to 3 dozen rolls.

POPPY SEED ROLLS

1. Shape dough for All-Purpose Rolls as desired.
2. Brush tops of rolls with egg white beaten only until frothy.
3. Sprinkle tops with poppy seed. Bake as directed in the recipe for All-Purpose Rolls.

Yield: 2-1/2 to 3 dozen rolls.

HOW TO SHAPE ROLLS

CLOVER LEAF ROLLS

1. Shape small pieces of dough in 3/4-inch balls, and dip each in melted butter or margarine.
2. Place 3 balls in each cup of a muffin pan.

CRESCENTS

1. Roll dough in a rectangle 1/4 inch thick.
2. With a floured knife, cut dough into 3-inch squares. Cut each square in half diagonally and brush with melted butter.
3. Roll each triangle of dough from the wide edge (base) to the point. Press point down firmly, and bring the 2 ends almost together to form a crescent.
4. Place rolls on greased cooky sheets. Brush with egg white beaten only until frothy with 2 tablespoons water.

BUTTERHORNS

1. Roll dough into an 8- or 9-inch circle about 1/4 inch thick, and cut into 10 or 12 pie-shaped wedges. Dip each wedge in melted butter or margarine and roll as for jelly roll, beginning from the wide edge.
2. Place rolls 1 inch apart on cooky sheets.

PARKER HOUSE ROLLS OR POCKETBOOK ROLLS

1. Roll dough 1/4 inch thick, cut with a floured 2- or 2-1/2-inch cooky cutter.
2. Make a crease just off center of each biscuit with the back of a knife blade.

3. Brush with melted butter or margarine, and fold each over so that the top half overlaps the bottom half in pocketbook fashion. Press edges together at the ends of the crease. Place on greased cooky sheets.

HOT ONION ROLLS

1 package (13 to 14 ounces) hot roll mix

1/3 cup instant minced onion

1/3 cup water

3 tablespoons butter or margarine, melted

1. Prepare hot roll mix according to package directions and let the dough rise one time.
2. Mix instant minced onion and water; let mixture stand 5 minutes to soften. Drain off all excess water.
3. Roll the dough on a lightly floured surface into a 11 x 5 x 1/2-inch rectangle.
4. Brush surface of dough with melted butter or margarine.
5. Sprinkle with the instant minced onion.
6. Roll up the dough in jelly-roll fashion, rolling the long side.
7. Cut the dough into slices 1/2 inch thick and place the cut slices on a lightly greased baking sheet.
8. Let the rolls rise, and bake them according to package directions.

Yield: 20 rolls.

HOT ONION HARD ROLLS

1/3 cup (3/4 stick) butter or margarine, softened

1/4 teaspoon onion powder

8 hard rolls

1. Combine butter or margarine and onion powder until creamy.
2. Split the rolls in half. Spread the cut sides with the onion butter.
3. Put 2 halves together, wrap in foil, and heat in a preheated moderate oven until rolls are hot.

Oven temperature: 350° to 375°F. (moderate).

Baking time: 10 to 15 minutes.

Yield: 8 rolls.

HOT GARLIC HARD ROLLS

Replace onion powder in the preceding recipe with 1/16 teaspoon instant minced garlic.

CHEESY FAN ROLLS

1 package (10 biscuits) ready-to-cook biscuits

1/4 cup butter or margarine, melted

1/2 cup grated sharp Cheddar cheese

1. Divide each ready-to-cook biscuit in half, using the fingers, to make 20 small biscuits.
2. Cut each small biscuit in half crosswise.
3. Dip each half biscuit in melted butter or margarine, and then dredge each in grated Cheddar cheese.
4. Stack 3 half biscuits in lightly buttered 2-1/2-inch muffin cups, having the round side of the biscuits up.

5. Bake in a preheated hot oven until biscuits have browned.
Oven temperature: 425°F. (hot).
Baking time: 12 to 15 minutes.
Yield: 13 fan rolls.

JIFFY ORANGE ROLLS

3 tablespoons butter or margarine

1/4 cup firmly packed light brown sugar

2 teaspoons grated orange rind

1/2 teaspoon grated lemon rind

1 tablespoon orange juice

1 dozen brown-and-serve rolls

1. Melt the butter or margarine in an 8 x 8 x 2-inch pan.
2. Add the next 4 ingredients, mix well, and spread the mixture over the bottom of the pan.
3. Arrange the brown-and-serve rolls over the mixture.
4. Bake in a preheated hot oven until the rolls have browned.
Oven temperature: 400°F. (hot).
Baking time: 15 minutes.
Yield: 12 rolls.

SEASONED CROUTONS

5 slices firm-textured white bread

3 tablespoons butter or margarine, melted

1 teaspoon imported paprika

1/8 teaspoon onion powder

1. Trim crusts from bread. Cut slices into 1/2-inch cubes.
2. Combine the remaining ingredients in a 1-quart mixing bowl, add bread cubes and mix well to coat them on all sides with the seasoned butter.
3. Turn cubes into an 11-1/2 x 7 x 1-1/2-inch baking pan.
4. Toast croutons in a preheated very hot oven until they are brown and dry, turning twice to toast uniformly.
5. Serve on soup, tossed green salads, or toss with melted butter or margarine and serve over cooked vegetables.

Oven temperature: 450°F. (very hot).

Baking time: 12 to 15 minutes.

Yield: 2 cups.

TOASTED CINNAMON STICKS

Quick to make and delicious with afternoon tea or coffee.

4 slices firm-textured bread   1/4 cup sugar
3 tablespoons butter or margarine, melted   1 teaspoon ground cinnamon

1. Cut crusts from bread, and cut each slice into 3 lengthwise strips.
2. Dip the bread strips in melted butter or margarine.
3. Combine sugar and cinnamon in a pie plate and roll the strips in the mixture.
4. Place the strips on a foil-lined cooky sheet and bake until they have browned and are crisp.

Oven temperature: 375°F. (moderate).

Baking time: 10 to 15 minutes.

Yield: 12 strips.

CAKES AND FROSTINGS

MY FAVORITE APPLESAUCE CAKE

Since this cake mellows with age, make it 2 to 3 days before serving.

2 cups sifted all-purpose flour

2 teaspoons soda
1 teaspoon salt
1 teaspoon ground cinnamon
1 teaspoon ground cloves
1 teaspoon ground nutmeg
1-1/4 cups light brown sugar, free from lumps and firmly packed

1-1/2 cups (15-ounce jar) sweetened applesauce
1/3 cup shortening
2 large eggs
2 tablespoons milk
1 cup chopped pecans
1 cup seedless raisins

Vanilla-Coffee Frosting

1. Reserve 1/4 cup of the flour. Sift remaining 1-3/4 cups flour with the next 6 ingredients. Set aside.
2. Heat applesauce and shortening together in a heat-proof mixing bowl. (Do not boil.)

44

3. Remove from heat and stir in 1-1/2 cups of the flour mixture. Beat in eggs, one at a time.
4. Gradually stir in remaining flour mixture and milk.
5. Coat pecans and raisins with reserved 1/4 cup flour, and add to the batter. Mix well. (If raisins are dry, rinse them with hot water. Drain well.)
6. Turn batter into 2 well-greased, lightly floured, round 9-inch layer-cake pans.
7. Bake in a preheated moderate oven until a cake tester inserted in the center comes out clean.
8. Turn cakes out onto wire racks to cool.
9. Spread Vanilla-Coffee Frosting in between layers and over top and sides of cake.

Oven temperature: 350°F. (moderate).
Baking time: 30 minutes.
Yield: 1 9-inch 2-layer cake or 16 servings.

MY BEST ANGEL FOOD CAKE

1-1/4 cups sifted cake flour
1-1/2 cups granulated sugar, sifted
1/2 teaspoon salt
1-1/2 cups (10 to 12) large egg whites

1-1/2 teaspoons cream of tartar
2-1/2 teaspoons vanilla extract
1/2 teaspoon almond extract (optional)

1. Sift flour and sugar together 6 times and set aside.
2. Add salt to egg whites and beat until frothy.
3. Add cream of tartar and beat egg whites until they stand in soft, stiff peaks when beater is withdrawn.

4. Add vanilla extract and almond extract, if used, and 1/4 cup of the flour mixture, and carefully fold into the beaten egg whites, using a rubber spatula.

5. Gently fold in the remaining flour mixture, 1/4 cup at a time, using about 15 strokes for each addition, and gently turning the bowl a little each time.

6. Rinse a 10 x 4-inch tube cake pan with cold water and drain it well.

7. Turn batter into the pan. Run a rubber spatula through the batter 3 or 4 times to remove any large air bubbles that might be in the batter.

8. Place cake in a cold oven. Set oven control to 300°F.

9. Bake 1-1/4 hours or until a cake tester inserted in the center comes out clean.

10. Remove cake from oven and invert it over a wire rack to cool, about 2 hours.

11. When cool, carefully loosen cake from the sides of pan with a spatula. Invert cake on a wire rack and lift off the pan.

12. Serve cake plain, sift confectioners' sugar over the top, or top with strawberries or other fruit and whipped cream. If desired, frost with fluffy Seven-Minute Frosting.

Oven temperature: 300°F. (slow).

Baking time: 1-1/4 hours.

Yield: 1 10-inch tube cake.

COCONUT LOAF CAKE

A cake rich in calories, but oh, so good! To save labor and time mix the first part of this cake with the electric mixer.

1 teaspoon double-acting baking powder
3 cups sifted all-purpose flour
1-1/2 cups (3 sticks) butter or margarine, softened
1/2 teaspoon salt
3/4 teaspoon almond extract
2 teaspoons vanilla extract
2 cups sugar
5 large eggs
1 cup milk
1 can (7 ounces) flaked coconut
Sugar Syrup

1. Sift baking powder with flour. Set aside.
2. Put the next 4 ingredients in the large bowl of the electric mixer and gradually blend in sugar, beating at medium speed for 5 minutes.
3. Beat in eggs, one at a time.
4. Add flour mixture, 1/2 cup at a time, alternately with milk, mixing by hand with a wooden spoon.
5. Fold in coconut.
6. Turn batter into a well-greased, lightly floured 10 x 4-inch tube cake pan.
7. Put cake in a cold oven, set oven control to 300°F. (slow), and bake until a cake tester inserted in the center of the cake comes out clean.
8. Remove cake from oven and, while hot, spoon Sugar Syrup over the top, using all the syrup.
9. Cool cake in the pan. When cake is cold, turn it out onto a large cake plate. Store in an airtight cake box.

Oven temperature: 300°F. (slow).
Baking time: 2 hours.
Yield: 1 loaf cake, 10 x 4 inches.

EASY CHOCOLATE CAKE

A delicate-textured cake, easy to make with an electric beater or in an electric mixer.

1 cup sifted all-purpose flour
1 cup sugar
5 tablespoons cocoa
1/4 teaspoon salt
1-1/2 teaspoons double-acting baking powder

1/3 cup (3/4 stick) butter or margarine, softened
2 large eggs
1/2 cup milk
1-1/2 teaspoons vanilla extract

Broiled Coconut Topping

1. Sift the first 5 ingredients in a 2-1/2 quart mixing bowl or in the larger bowl of an electric mixer.
2. Add the next 4 ingredients.
3. Beat 3 minutes by the clock with an electric beater (hand electric beater or electric mixer).
4. Turn the batter into a well-greased, lightly floured, 8 x 8 x 2-inch pan.
5. Bake in a preheated moderate oven until a cake tester or toothpick inserted in the center comes out clean.
6. While cake is still hot, spread Broiled Coconut Topping over the top.
7. Place the cake in the broiler oven with oven control set to broil for 2 to 3 minutes or until the topping has browned lightly, being careful not to burn the topping.
8. Serve from the pan, cut into squares.

Oven temperature: 350°F. (moderate).
Baking time: 40 minutes.
Yield: 9 servings or 1 8-inch square cake.

EASY CHOCOLATE LAYER CAKE

Bake Easy Chocolate Cake in 2 well-greased, lightly floured, round, 8-inch layer-cake pans in a preheated moderate oven until a toothpick or cake tester inserted in the center comes out clean. Cool cake in pans 10 minutes. Then turn out onto cooling racks to finish cooling. When cold, spread Easy Chocolate Frosting between layers and over the top and sides.
Oven temperature: 350°F.
Baking time: 25 to 30 minutes.
Yield: 12 servings.

BROWN-SUGAR CHOCOLATE CAKE

2/3 cup shortening
1 teaspoon soda
1/2 teaspoon salt
2 teaspoons vanilla extract
_____
1-1/4 cups dark brown sugar, firmly packed
3 squares (3 ounces) unsweetened chocolate, melted and cooled

2 large eggs
1-1/2 cups sifted all-purpose flour
2/3 cup buttermilk or sour milk
_____
Mocha Frosting

1. Put the first 4 ingredients in a mixing bowl; mix well.
2. Press out all lumps in the brown sugar, and gradually blend it with shortening mixture.
3. Stir in melted, cooled chocolate.
4. Beat in eggs, one at a time.
5. Add flour, 1/2 cup at a time, alternating with 1/3 cup buttermilk or sour milk, beginning and ending with flour.

6. Beat batter 1/2 minute. Then turn it into 2 well-greased, lightly floured, round, 8-inch layer-cake pans.

9. Bake until a toothpick inserted in the center comes out clean.

10. Cool cakes in pans 10 minutes. Then remove them from the pans onto wire racks to finish cooling.

11. Spread Mocha Frosting between the layers and over the top and sides of the cake. Store airtight.

Oven temperature: 375°F. (moderate).

Baking time: 25 minutes.

Yield: One 2-layer, round 8-inch cake or 12 servings.

BUTTER-PECAN CAKE

3 tablespoons butter or margarine

1 cup chopped pecans

2 cups sifted all-purpose flour

2 teaspoons double-acting baking powder

3/4 cup (1-1/2 sticks) butter or margarine, softened

1/4 teaspoon salt

2 teaspoons vanilla extract

2 large eggs

3/4 cup milk

Browned-Butter Frosting

16 whole pecan halves (optional)

1. Melt the 3 tablespoons butter or margarine in a 2-quart saucepan, add pecans, and stir and cook over moderate heat 3 to 4 minutes. Cool.

2. Sift flour with baking powder. Set aside.

3. Put the next 3 ingredients in a 2-1/2-quart mixing bowl. Mix well. Beat in eggs, one at a time.

4. Stir in cooled, buttered pecans.
5. Add flour mixture alternately with milk. Beat batter 1/2 minute.
6. Turn batter into 2 well-greased, lightly floured, round 9-inch layer-cake pans.
7. Bake in a preheated moderate oven until a cake tester or toothpick inserted in the center comes out clean.
8. Cool cakes in pans 10 minutes. Turn cakes onto wire racks to finish cooling.
9. Spread Browned-Butter Frosting between layers and over the top and sides. Garnish the top with whole pecan halves if desired.

Oven temperature: 350° F. (moderate).

Baking time: 35 minutes.

Yield: 1 9-inch, 2-layer cake.

COTTAGE PUDDING

1-3/4 cups sifted all-purpose flour

2 teaspoons double-acting baking powder

1/4 teaspoon salt

1/3 cup (3/4 stick) butter or margarine, softened

1 cup sugar

1 large egg, at room temperature

3/4 cup milk

1-1/2 teaspoons vanilla extract

Lemon Cream Topping, Chocolate, Orange Dessert, or Fresh Strawberry Sauce

1. Sift flour, baking powder, and salt together into a 2-1/2-quart mixing bowl. Set aside.

2. Put the next 5 ingredients in the blender container and blend until smooth, about 1 minute. If you do not own an electric blender, make this cake using the creaming method of mixing cakes.

3. Pour blended ingredients gradually over sifted ingredients, stirring quickly but thoroughly until just mixed.

4. Turn the batter into a well-greased, lightly floured, 8 x 8 x 2-inch baking pan.

5. Bake in a preheated moderate oven until a toothpick or cake tester inserted in the center comes out clean.

6. Cool 10 minutes in the pan. Turn out on a cooling rack to finish cooling, if desired.

7. Serve warm or cold, cut into squares, with the desired topping.

Oven temperature: 350°F. (moderate).

Baking time: 45 minutes.

Yield: 9 servings.

EVERY-OCCASION YELLOW CAKE

A light, fine-textured yellow cake suitable for all occasions.

2 cups sifted cake flour

2 teaspoons double-acting baking powder

1/2 teaspoon salt

1/2 cup shortening

1 teaspoon vanilla extract

1/2 teaspoon almond extract (optional)

1 cup sugar

2 large whole eggs plus 1 large egg yolk

3/4 cup milk

Seven-Minute Frosting or any other frosting desired

1. Sift the first 3 ingredients together and set aside.
2. Mix shortening with vanilla and almond extracts.
3. Gradually add sugar, mixing well after each addition.
4. Beat in whole eggs, one at a time, and egg yolk.
5. Stir in flour mixture alternately with milk.
6. Beat batter 1/2 minute.
7. Turn batter into 2 well-greased, lightly floured, 8-inch, round cake pans.
8. Bake in a preheated moderate oven until a cake tester or toothpick inserted in the center comes out clean.
9. Cool cakes in pans 10 minutes. Then turn cakes onto wire racks to finish cooling.
10. Frost cakes with Seven-Minute Frosting or any other frosting desired, spreading it between layers, and over top and sides.

Oven temperature: 375°F. (moderate).
Baking time: 25 to 30 minutes.
Yield: One 2-layer, round, 8-inch cake (12 servings).

JAVA COCONUT CAKE

Recipe for Every-Occasion
   Yellow Cake
1-3/4 teaspoons instant coffee
Brown Sugar–Marshmallow
   Frosting

1 cup shredded coconut or
   flaked coconut

1. Make the recipe for Every-Occasion Yellow Cake, omitting almond extract, and adding the instant coffee to the shortening.

2. When cake is baked and is cold, frost with Brown Sugar Marshmallow Frosting, sprinkling coconut over frosting between layers, and over frosting on top and sides of cake. Yield: One 2-layer, 8-inch cake (12 servings).

HOT MILK CAKE

1 cup sifted all-purpose flour
1/2 teaspoon salt
1/2 teaspoon soda
1 teaspoon cream of tartar
_____
2 large eggs
3/4 cup sugar
_____

1 tablespoon butter or margarine
3/4 teaspoon lemon extract or vanilla extract
1/2 cup hot milk
_____
Easy Caramel Frosting (optional)

1. Sift the first 4 ingredients together. Set aside.
2. Break eggs into a 2-quart mixing bowl, and with an electric beater beat 2 to 3 minutes, or beat with a rotary beater for 5 minutes.
3. Gradually beat in sugar. Beat with an electric beater 2 to 3 minutes, or with a rotary beater 5 minutes.
4. Add butter or margarine and lemon extract or vanilla extract to hot milk. Mix until butter is melted. Then add mixture to beaten eggs and sugar, alternating with flour mixture, beginning and ending with flour.
5. Turn batter into a well-greased, lightly floured 8 x 8 x 2-inch pan, or into well-greased and lightly floured or paper-lined 1-3/4- x 1-inch cupcake pans.

6. Bake in a moderate oven until a cake tester or toothpick inserted in the center comes out clean.
7. Turn cake or cupcakes onto wire racks to cool.
8. Frost with Easy Caramel Frosting or with any frosting desired, or serve plain.

Oven temperature: 350°F. (moderate).

Baking time: 8 x 8 x 2-inch cake 35 minutes; cupcakes about 20 minutes.

Yield: 1 cake, 8 x 8 x 2 inches, or about 18 cupcakes.

RICH FRUIT CAKE

1-1/2 cups shortening
1 teaspoon soda
1-1/2 teaspoons salt
1 teaspoon ground cinnamon
1 teaspoon ground nutmeg

1 cup sugar
3/4 cup unsulphured molasses

4 cups sifted all-purpose flour
5 large eggs, unbeaten
4 cups mixed diced candied fruit
2 cups seedless raisins
1-1/2 cups coarsely chopped pecans

1. Line a greased 10-inch tube cake pan with brown paper cut to fit the bottom of the pan. Grease paper and flour it lightly. Set pan aside.
2. Put the first 5 ingredients in a 4-quart mixing bowl and mix well. Gradually blend in sugar and molasses.
3. Stir in 1 cup of the flour.
4. Beat in eggs, one at a time.
5. Add the remaining 3 cups flour gradually, about 1/2 cup at a time.

6. Stir in candied fruit, raisins, and pecans.
7. Turn dough into the prepared tube cake pan.
8. Bake in a preheated slow oven until a cake tester inserted in the center comes out clean.
9. Keep a large shallow pan of hot water on rack underneath the cake while it is baking.
10. Cool cake completely in the pan.
11. Turn cake out of the pan, remove paper from the bottom, and wrap cake in foil or plastic wrap.
12. Store cake in an airtight cake box or other container.

Oven temperature: 300°F. (slow).

Baking time: 3 hours.

Yield: One 7-pound fruit cake.

RICH FUDGE CAKE

A delicious brownie-like cake that needs no frosting or other embellishment.

1/2 cup (1 stick) butter or margarine
2 squares (2 ounces) unsweetened chocolate
1 cup sugar
2 large eggs, beaten

1 teaspoon vanilla extract
2 cups pecans, coarsely chopped
1/2 cup sifted all-purpose flour

1. Line the bottom of a greased 8 x 8 x 2-inch pan with brown paper or with heavy wax paper, cut to fit the bottom. Grease paper and set pan aside.
2. Put butter or margarine and chocolate in the top of a 2-

quart double boiler and place over simmering water to melt. Remove top of double boiler from heat.

3. Add sugar and mix well.
4. Stir in eggs and vanilla extract.
5. Add pecans and flour. Mix until all ingredients are well blended.
6. Spread dough in the prepared baking pan.
7. Bake in a preheated slow oven until a toothpick or cake tester inserted in the center comes out clean.
8. Cool cake in the pan 20 minutes. Then turn out onto a wire rack to finish cooling, top side up.
9. When cake is cold, cut it into 9 or 12 pieces.

Oven temperature: 325°F. (slow).
Baking time: 40 minutes.
Yield: 9 to 12 pieces.

QUICK GINGERBREAD

Delicious and easy as one, two, three, to make.

2 cups sifted all-purpose flour
1/3 cup sugar
1 teaspoon double-acting baking powder
1/2 teaspoon soda
1/2 teaspoon salt
2 teaspoons ground cinnamon
1-1/2 teaspoons ground ginger

1 cup sugar-cane syrup or unsulphured molasses
1/2 cup buttermilk or sour milk
1 large egg
1/2 cup (1 stick) butter or margarine, melted
1/4 cup hot water

1. Sift the first 7 ingredients together into a 2-1/2-quart mixing bowl.
2. Stir in the next 4 ingredients and mix well.
3. Beat in hot water.
4. Pour the batter into a well-greased, lightly floured 9 x 9 x 2-inch baking pan.
5. Bake in a preheated moderate oven until a toothpick inserted in the center comes out clean.
6. Serve hot or cold with whipped cream or Lemon Cream Topping.

Oven temperature: 350°F. (moderate).

Baking time: 45 minutes.

Yield: 9 to 12 servings.

REFRIGERATOR GINGERBREAD CUPCAKES

1/2 cup (1 stick) butter or margarine, softened

1 teaspoon soda

1 teaspoon ground ginger

1 teaspoon ground cinnamon

1/2 cup sugar

2 large eggs

1/2 cup sugar-cane syrup or unsulphured molasses

1/2 cup chopped pecans

1/2 cup seedless raisins or chopped dried dates

1-3/4 cups sifted all-purpose flour

1/2 cup buttermilk or sour milk

1. Put the first 5 ingredients in a mixing bowl and mix until well blended.
2. Beat in eggs. Stir in sugar-cane syrup or molasses.
3. Mix pecans, raisins or dates, and flour and add the mixture,

1/2 cup at a time, alternately with buttermilk or sour milk to sugar and butter mixture. Beat the batter 1/2 minute.

4. Store batter in a covered bowl in the refrigerator. Bake it as needed in paper-lined cupcake pans, filling them 2/3 full with batter.

5. Bake in a preheated moderate oven until a toothpick or cake tester inserted in the center comes out clean.

6. Serve plain or with whipped cream, Lemon Cream Topping, or Orange Dessert Sauce.

Oven temperature: 350°F. (moderate).

Baking time: 25 minutes.

Yield: 1-1/2 dozen cupcakes.

MINCEMEAT CAKE

This moist, easy-to-make cake is almost as delicious as fruit cake.

2-1/2 cups sifted all-purpose flour

3 teaspoons double-acting baking powder

1/4 teaspoon salt

1/2 cup (1 stick) butter or margarine, softened

2 teaspoons vanilla extract

1 cup sugar

2 large eggs

1-3/4 cups moist mincemeat

1. Cut a piece of brown paper to fit the bottom of a 9-1/2 x 5 x 3-inch loaf pan. Grease the bottom of the loaf pan, place brown paper over the bottom, and press it down well. Grease paper and set pan aside.

2. Sift the first 3 ingredients together and set aside.

3. Put butter or margarine and vanilla extract in a 2-1/2-quart mixing bowl and mix well.
4. Gradually blend in sugar, 1/4 cup at a time.
5. Beat in eggs, one at a time.
6. Stir in mincemeat.
7. Gradually add flour mixture, 1/2 cup at a time, mixing well after each addition.
8. Turn batter into the prepared loaf pan.
9. Bake in a preheated oven until a cake tester inserted in the center comes out clean.
10. Cool cake in pan 20 minutes. Then turn cake out onto a wire rack to finish cooling.
11. Wrap cake in foil and store in an airtight container.

Oven temperature: 325°F. (slow).

Baking time: 1-1/4 hours.

Yield: 1 cake, 9-1/2 x 5 x 3 inches.

POUND CAKE

The only leavening agent in genuine pound cake is the air beaten into the batter. The electric beater or mixer makes this job a little easier. In addition, the cake is larger.

1 cup (2 sticks) butter or margarine, softened

1-1/2 teaspoons ground mace or nutmeg

2 teaspoons vanilla extract

1/2 teaspoon salt (optional)

1-2/3 cups sugar

6 large eggs, at room temperature

2 cups sifted all-purpose flour

1. Put the first 4 ingredients in large bowl of the electric mixer or in a 2-1/2-quart mixing bowl.

2. At low speed, mix the ingredients until well blended.
3. At medium speed, beat in sugar, 1/3 cup at a time, beating well after each addition.
4. At high speed, beat in 5 of the eggs, one at a time, beating well after each addition. (Reserve 1 egg for later use.)
5. With a wooden mixing spoon, stir in flour, 1/4 cup at a time.
6. Beat in the remaining egg.
7. Grease the bottom (not sides) of a 9 x 3-1/2-inch round tube cake pan. Turn dough into the pan.
8. Place cake in a cold oven. Turn oven control to 300°F. (slow). Bake 1-1/2 hours or until a cake tester inserted in the center comes out clean. Cool in pan 20 minutes. Turn out onto a wire rack to finish cooling.

Oven temperature: 300°F. (slow).

Baking time: 1-1/2 hours.

Yield: 1 9-inch tube cake.

SPONGE CAKE

6 large eggs, separated

1-1/4 cups sugar
3/4 teaspoon ground mace
1 teaspoon grated lemon rind
1 tablespoon grated orange rind

1 tablespoon lemon juice
1/2 teaspoon salt
1-1/2 cups sifted cake flour
confectioners' sugar or Lemon Cream Topping

1. Beat egg yolks until they are thick and lemon colored.
2. Gradually beat in the next 4 ingredients, beating well after each addition.

3. Beat in lemon juice.
4. Add salt to egg whites, and beat until whites are stiff but not dry. Pile on top of yolk mixture.
5. Sift flour, all at once, over egg whites, and carefully fold egg whites and flour into yolk mixture.
6. Rinse a 10 x 4-inch tube cake pan with cold water, drain well, but do not dry.
7. Turn cake batter into the pan.
8. Bake in a preheated slow oven until cake has browned and pulls away from sides of pan.
9. Invert cake (still in pan) on a wire rack and cool.
10. Loosen cake from sides of pan and from sides of center tube with a spatula. Invert cake on a wire rack, and lift off the pan.
11. Sift confectioners' sugar lightly over the top.

Oven temperature: 325°F. (slow).

Baking time: Approximately 1 hour.

Yield: 1 10-inch tube cake.

PASSOVER SPONGE CAKE

6 large eggs, separated
1 large whole egg
1/4 teaspoon salt
1-1/2 cups sugar

1-1/2 tablespoons lemon juice
1 teaspoon grated lemon rind
3/4 cup sifted potato starch
sifted confectioners' sugar

1. Put egg yolks, whole egg, and salt in a 2-1/2 quart mixing bowl. Beat with a rotary or electric beater until eggs are foamy.
2. Gradually beat in sugar, 2 tablespoons at a time.

3. Beat in lemon juice and lemon rind. Continue beating until eggs are thick and light lemon colored.
4. Carefully blend in potato starch, 1/4 cup at a time.
5. Beat egg whites until they are stiff enough to form soft, stiff peaks that bend over slightly when beater is withdrawn.
6. Add egg whites, all at one time, and gently fold them into the batter.
7. Rinse a round 10 x 4-inch tube cake pan in cold water and drain it well. (Do not dry.)
8. Pour batter into the pan. Bake until cake is firm in the center.
9. Cool cake in pan. Loosen the cake from sides of pan with a spatula and turn it out onto a wire rack or serving plate, having the top side up.
10. Sift confectioners' sugar over the top.

Oven temperature: 350°F. (moderate).

Baking time: 50 to 60 minutes.

Yield: 1 10-inch, round loaf cake or 12 to 16 servings.

FROSTINGS

BROWNED-BUTTER FROSTING

1/2 cup (1 stick) butter or margarine

2-1/2 cups sifted confectioners' sugar

2 tablespoons light corn syrup, maple syrup, or sugar-cane syrup

3 tablespoons undiluted evaporated milk or light cream

1 teaspoon vanilla extract

1. Put butter or margarine in a heat-proof, 2-quart saucepan and melt over moderate low heat.
2. Continue cooking until butter or margarine is straw color. Remove from heat and cool.
3. Add confectioners' sugar alternately with syrup and milk or cream. At first, frosting will appear grainy; stir and beat 3 to 4 minutes, and it will become smooth.
4. Stir in vanilla extract. Spread frosting between 2 cake layers and over top and sides.

Yield: Frosting for 2-layer, 9-inch cake.

BROWN SUGAR-MARSHMALLOW FROSTING

1 large egg white, unbeaten
3/4 cup light brown sugar
2 teaspoons light corn syrup
1/4 cup water
1/16 teaspoon salt

1-1/2 teaspoons vanilla extract

1/2 cup snipped marshmallows or miniature marshmallows

1. Put the first 6 ingredients in the top of a double boiler, mix well, and place over the bottom of a double boiler filled with boiling water to a depth of about 2 inches.
2. Place double boiler over medium-high heat. Beat with an electric beater, at high speed, until frosting stands in stiff peaks.
3. Remove frosting from heat, add marshmallows, and continue beating until frosting stands in very stiff peaks.
4. Spread over cold cake.

Yield: Frosting for an 8-inch 2-layer cake.

EASY CARAMEL FROSTING

1/4 cup (1/2 stick) butter or margarine

1/3 cup dark brown sugar

1-1/2 tablespoons milk or light cream

about 1 cup sifted confectioners' sugar

3/4 teaspoon vanilla extract

1. Melt butter or margarine in a 1-quart saucepan.
2. Add brown sugar, mix well, and cook, stirring, over low heat for 1-1/2 minutes.
3. Add milk or light cream and bring the mixture to boiling point, stirring constantly.
4. Remove saucepan from the heat and gradually stir in confectioners' sugar and vanilla extract.
5. Beat frosting 1 to 2 minutes or until frosting is of spreading consistency, adding a little more confectioners' sugar if frosting is not stiff enough. (If frosting becomes firm before it can be spread over the cake, thin with a few drops milk or cream.)

Yield: Frosting for top and sides of a square 8 x 8 x 2-inch cake or 18 cupcakes.

EASY CHOCOLATE FROSTING

1 cup (6-ounce package) semi-sweet chocolate pieces

1/2 cup undiluted evaporated milk

1 teaspoon vanilla extract

3 cups sifted confectioners' sugar

1. Put semi-sweet chocolate pieces and evaporated milk in a 2-quart saucepan.
2. Stir and cook over low heat until chocolate is melted.
3. Remove saucepan from heat and add vanilla extract and confectioners' sugar. Stir and beat until frosting is smooth.
4. Spread frosting between layers and over top and sides of cake. Store airtight.

Yield: Frosting for tops and sides of an 8-inch 2-layer cake or top of a 9-inch 2-layer cake.

SEVEN-MINUTE FROSTING

1 large egg white, unbeaten
3/4 cup sugar
1/16 teaspoon salt
1/4 cup water
2 teaspoons light corn syrup

or 1/4 teaspoon cream of tartar
1-1/2 teaspoons vanilla extract or 1/2 teaspoon almond extract

1. Put all ingredients in the top of a double boiler, mix well, and place over the bottom of the double boiler filled with boiling water to a depth of 2 inches. Place over medium-high heat.
2. Beat mixture with an electric beater, at high speed, 7 minutes or until frosting stands in stiff peaks, keeping the water boiling rapidly.
3. Remove double boiler from the heat, and continue beating until frosting stands in very stiff peaks.
4. Spread frosting over cold cake.

Yield: Frosting for an 8-inch 2-layer cake.

MOCHA FROSTING

6 tablespoons butter

1 tablespoon light corn syrup

3 cups sifted confectioners' sugar

4 to 5 tablespoons light cream or undiluted evaporated milk

1 teaspoon instant coffee

1-1/2 teaspoons vanilla extract

1 square (1 ounce) unsweetened chocolate, melted and cooled

1. Heat butter in a 1-quart saucepan until it is golden.
2. Stir in corn syrup.
3. Add confectioners' sugar and enough light cream or undiluted evaporated milk to make a frosting that is smooth and can be spread easily.
4. Blend in remaining 3 ingredients.

Yield: Frosting for top and sides of two round 8-inch cake layers.

VANILLA-COFFEE FROSTING

1/2 cup (1 stick) butter or margarine, softened

3/4 teaspoon instant coffee

2 teaspoons vanilla extract

2 cups sifted confectioners' sugar

1 tablespoon milk or light cream

1. Put the first 3 ingredients in a 1-1/2-quart mixing bowl and mix until fluffy.
2. Gradually stir in sugar and milk. Mix until smooth.

3. Spread frosting between layers and over top and sides of cake.

Yield: Frosting for between layers and over top and sides of a 2-layer 9-inch cake.

LEMON CREAM TOPPING

2 large egg yolks, beaten until light and lemon colored

1/4 teaspoon ground mace or ground nutmeg

1/4 teaspoon grated lemon rind

1/4 teaspoon vanilla extract

1/2 cup sifted confectioners' sugar

1 tablespoon lemon juice

3/4 cup heavy cream, whipped

1. Combine the first 4 ingredients in a 1-quart mixing bowl. Mix well.
2. Gradually beat in confectioners' sugar and lemon juice.
3. Fold in whipped cream. Serve as a topping for Sponge Cake or Cottage Pudding.

Yield: Approximately 1-1/2 cups.

SUGAR SYRUP

1 cup sugar

1/2 cup water

1/4 cup light corn syrup

3 tablespoons butter or margarine

1/2 teaspoon vanilla extract

1. Mix the first 4 ingredients in a small saucepan. Bring to boiling point and boil gently 5 minutes.
2. Add vanilla extract. Spoon over warm cake.

CHEESE AND EGG DISHES

Cheese and eggs combine nicely with most other foods to make many hot dishes, salads, sandwiches, desserts, etc. They should be cooked at a low temperature (a temperature below that of boiling water). If cooked at high temperature, eggs will become tough and cheese will become tough and stringy. Both cheese and eggs keep best stored at refrigerator temperature. The best container for storing eggs is the carton in which they are packed for the market. Cheese should be wrapped in plastic wrap or aluminum foil.

BAKED HAM AND EGGS

Serve for lunch or supper with Broiled Peaches.

1-1/2 pounds uncooked ham, sliced 1/4 inch thick

6 large eggs

1/2 teaspoon salt

1/4 teaspoon ground black pepper

3 tablespoons fine dry bread-crumbs

6 teaspoons butter or margarine

snipped parsley

69

1. Cut ham into 6 serving-size pieces and arrange them in a lightly buttered 13 x 9 x 2-inch baking dish or in 6 individual casseroles.
2. Break an egg over each serving.
3. Sprinkle salt, black pepper, and 1-1/2 teaspoons of the bread-crumbs over each egg.
4. Dot each with 1 teaspoon butter or margarine.
5. Bake in a moderate oven until egg whites have set.
6. Transfer ham and eggs to a warmed platter or serve in the individual baking dishes.
7. Garnish with snipped parsley.

Oven temperature: 325°F. (slow).

Baking time: 25 to 30 minutes.

Yield: 6 servings.

BANANAS IN BACON BLANKETS WITH BAKED EGGS

A perfect combination for brunch or supper.

4 medium-sized bananas, peeled and cut in half
1 tablespoon lemon juice
4 to 8 eggs
salt and ground black pepper to taste
8 slices bacon, cooked until half done
4 sprigs parsley

1. Break 1 or 2 eggs in each of 4 buttered oval-shaped individual baking dishes. Sprinkle with salt and pepper to taste.
2. Dip the bananas in the lemon juice to prevent discoloration.

3. Wrap each half banana in a strip of partially cooked bacon, and place 1 half at each end of the baking dishes.
4. Bake uncovered, in a preheated moderate oven until egg whites have set.
5. Garnish each serving with a sprig of parsley.
6. Serve with grapefruit or cantaloupe, hot biscuits or rolls with butter and strawberry preserves or orange marmalade.

Oven temperature: 350°F. (moderate).

Baking time: 15 to 20 minutes.

Yield: 4 servings.

BAKED CHEESE FONDUE

Here is a fine luncheon or supper dish that is easy to make for the family or guests. Serve it with crisp bacon, Molded Cranberry Salad and hot Green Beans with Tomato Mayonnaise, and French bread.

2 cups soft bread crumbs
1/2 teaspoon powdered mustard
1-1/2 cups milk
1-3/4 cups (7 ounces) grated sharp Cheddar cheese

3/4 teaspoon salt
dash cayenne
1 tablespoon butter or margarine, melted
3 large eggs, separated

1. Soak bread crumbs and mustard in the milk until crumbs have absorbed all the milk.
2. Add the next 4 ingredients. Mix well.
3. Beat egg yolks until light and lemon colored. Add to the mixture.

4. Beat egg whites until they stand in soft peaks (not dry) when beater is raised. Gently fold them into the mixture.
5. Turn the mixture into an ungreased 1-quart casserole or soufflé dish.
6. Place the casserole or soufflé dish in a pan of hot water and bake in a preheated slow oven until the fondue is well puffed and is soft-firm in the center. Serve promptly.

Oven temperature: 325°F. (slow).

Baking time: 1-1/4 hours.

Yield: 6 servings.

CHEESE SOUFFLÉ

1/4 cup (1/2 stick) butter or margarine

4 tablespoons flour

1/4 teaspoon salt

1 cup milk

1 cup (1/4 pound) finely shredded sharp Cheddar cheese

3 large eggs, separated

1 teaspoon powdered mustard soaked in 1 teaspoon water

dash cayenne

1/4 teaspoon ground black pepper

1/4 teaspoon cream of tartar

1. Melt butter or margarine in a 1-1/2-quart saucepan.
2. Remove pan from the heat and blend in flour.
3. Stir and cook until mixture is bubbly, 1/2 to 1 minute.
4. Remove from heat and beat in milk.
5. Stir and cook until the sauce is of medium thickness.
6. Add cheese and mix well.
7. Beat egg yolks until they are thick and lemon colored.

8. Add a little of the hot sauce to the egg yolks then stir the mixture into the remaining hot sauce.
9. Add the next 3 ingredients and mix.
10. Beat egg whites until foamy, add cream of tartar and beat until egg whites stand in soft stiff peaks.
11. Fold the cheese sauce into the beaten egg whites.
12. Turn the mixture into a 1-1/2-quart soufflé dish or casserole, having only bottom of dish buttered.
13. Place the dish in a pan of hot water. Bake in a preheated slow oven until the soufflé is well puffed and browned. Serve at once.

Oven temperature: 325°F. (slow).
Baking time: 1-1/4 hours.
Yield: 4 to 6 servings.

CHEESE PUFFS

Serve piping hot for lunch or supper with crisp bacon and fruit salad.

3 large eggs, separated
1/4 teaspoon ground black pepper
1-1/2 cups finely shredded sharp Cheddar cheese

dash salt
6 slices firm-textured bread, each slice buttered on one side

1. Put egg yolks in a 1-1/2-quart mixing bowl; beat well.
2. Stir in black pepper and cheese.
3. Add salt to egg whites and beat until the egg whites stand in soft, stiff peaks. Fold them gently into the mixture.

4. Place buttered slices of bread on a baking sheet and pile the mixture on the slices.

5. Bake in a preheated hot oven until the cheese mixture is well puffed. Serve promptly.

Oven temperature: 400°F. (hot).

Baking time: 12 to 15 minutes.

Yield: 6 servings.

CHILI WELSH RABBIT

1 can (10-1/2-ounces) condensed tomato soup

1 tablespoon minced green pepper

1/8 teaspoon salt or salt to taste

1/16 teaspoon ground black pepper

1-1/4 teaspoons chili powder

1 cup finely shredded sharp Cheddar cheese

6 slices toast

12 slices crisp bacon

1. Put the first 5 ingredients in a 1-1/2-quart saucepan and mix well.

2. Cook, stirring, until mixture begins to boil, 4 to 5 minutes.

3. Add the cheese and stir until all the cheese has melted.

4. Spoon mixture over toast slices and top each serving with 2 slices crisp bacon. Serve promptly.

Yield: 6 servings.

CREAMED EGGS ON
CHOW MEIN NOODLES

3 tablespoons butter or margarine

2 tablespoons finely chopped onion

3 tablespoons flour

1/2 teaspoon dried tarragon or dried marjoram (optional)

3/4 teaspoon salt

1/16 teaspoon ground black pepper

2 cups milk

1/2 cup shredded American cheese

6 hard-cooked eggs, sliced

chow mein noodles, heated

1. Melt butter or margarine in a 1-1/2-quart saucepan.
2. Add onion and cook 1 to 2 minutes or until soft.
3. Remove saucepan from the heat and stir in the next 4 ingredients. Return the saucepan to the heat and cook, stirring, until the mixture foams.
4. Remove saucepan from the heat and beat in milk. Stir and cook until the sauce is of medium thickness.
5. Add cheese and eggs and heat only until the cheese melts.
6. Serve over chow mein noodles for lunch or supper with Cabbage and Spinach Slaw.

Yield: 6 servings.

DEVILED EGGS

12 hard-cooked eggs

1/4 cup finely chopped celery

2 tablespoons finely chopped pimiento-stuffed green olives or gherkins

1 teaspoon salt or salt to taste

1 teaspoon prepared mustard

1/8 teaspoon ground black pepper

1/3 cup mayonnaise

chopped parsley, or paprika

1. Peel the eggs and cut them in half lengthwise.
2. Remove yolks and put them through a sieve, a few at a time.
3. Add the next 6 ingredients to the sieved yolks and mix well.
4. Using a teaspoon, put the mixture into the cavities of the egg whites. Or if desired, put the mixture in a pastry bag or cake decorator's tube and pipe it into the egg white cavities.
5. Sprinkle deviled eggs with chopped parsley or paprika.

Yield: 24 deviled egg halves.

POTATO OMELET

3 tablespoons butter or margarine

1 small onion, sliced thin

1 medium-sized potato, sliced thin

4 large eggs, beaten

1 tablespoon cold water or milk

1 teaspoon salt

1/8 teaspoon ground black pepper

chopped parsley, or paprika

1. Melt the butter or margarine in a heavy 8-inch skillet.
2. Add the sliced onion and potato, cover and cook over moderate heat only until soft. (Do not allow them to brown.)

3. Combine the eggs, water or milk, salt, and black pepper and pour the mixture over the onion and potato. Shake the skillet to allow the egg mixture to flow under the onion and potato.

4. Cook over low heat until eggs are set and the surface still moist.

5. Using a spatula, make a crease down the center of the omelet at right angle to the handle and fold the side of the omelet that is next to the handle of the skillet over the remaining side.

6. Turn the omelet out onto a warmed platter. Sprinkle with chopped parsley or paprika.

7. Serve with crisp bacon, Grilled Tomatoes, hot crisp rolls, and preserves or marmalade.

Yield: 3 servings.

COOKIES

The cookies in this chapter can be divided into six basic types: bar and square cookies, drop cookies, molded and shaped cookies, pressed cookies, refrigerator cookies, and rolled cookies.

ARMENIAN SUGAR COOKIES

1-1/2 teaspoons vanilla extract

2 cups (1 pound) unsalted butter, softened

2 cups sugar

4 cups sifted all-purpose flour

8 dozen blanched whole almonds

1. Blend vanilla extract with butter in a 2-1/2-quart bowl.
2. Stir in sugar, 1/4 cup at a time.
3. Add flour, 1/2 cup at a time, mixing well after each addition. (This dough is stiff, but do not add water or milk.)
4. Shape dough into 1-inch balls and place them on ungreased cooky sheets, about 1-1/2 inches apart.
5. Press a whole almond in the top of each ball.
6. Bake in a slow oven until cookies have browned lightly around the edges.

7. Cool on wire racks, and store in airtight containers.

Oven temperature: 325°F. (slow).

Baking time: 15 to 20 minutes.

Yield: About 8 dozen cookies.

BROWN SUGAR SPRITZ

1 cup (2 sticks) butter or margarine, softened

1/4 teaspoon salt

1-1/2 teaspoons vanilla extract

1/2 cup light brown sugar, firmly packed

1 large egg

2-1/4 cups sifted all-purpose flour

red and green granulated sugar for decorating

1. Put the first 3 ingredients in a mixing bowl. Mix well.
2. Press out all lumps from the brown sugar and gradually blend with the butter mixture.
3. Beat in egg.
4. Gradually stir in flour, about 1/4 cup at a time.
5. Put dough into a metal cooky press, with any plate desired Press dough onto ungreased cooky sheets, 2 inches apart to allow room for spreading.
6. Sprinkle cookies with red or green granulated sugar.
7. Bake in a preheated oven 7 to 10 minutes or until cookies have browned lightly around the edges.
8. Cool on wire rack. Store airtight.

Oven temperature: 375°F. (moderate).

Baking time: 7 to 10 minutes.

Yield: About 7 dozen.

BUTTER CRESCENTS

1 cup (2 sticks) butter or margarine
1/4 teaspoon salt
1-1/2 teaspoons vanilla extract

1/2 cup sugar
2-1/4 cups sifted all-purpose flour
sifted confectioners' sugar

1. Put the first 3 ingredients in a mixing bowl. Mix well.
2. Gradually blend in sugar.
3. Stir in flour, about 1/4 cup at a time. Dough will be stiff, but do not add liquid.
4. Chill dough until stiff enough to handle, 1 to 2 hours.
5. Pinch off 1-inch balls of dough; shape into crescents.
6. Place crescents on ungreased baking sheets and bake until lightly browned around the edges.
7. Remove from oven and transfer to cooling racks.
8. While still hot, roll them in sifted confectioners' sugar. Roll again in confectioners' sugar when cold. Store in airtight containers.

Oven temperature: 350°F. (moderate).
Baking time: 12 to 15 minutes.
Yield: 5 dozen cookies.

BUTTER BALLS:

Shape Butter Crescent dough into 1-inch balls. Continue as directed in the recipe.
Yield: 5 dozen cookies.

BUTTER-PECAN BALLS

1 cup (2 sticks) butter or margarine, softened

1/2 cup sugar

1-1/2 teaspoons vanilla extract

1 cup pecans, chopped medium-fine

2 cups sifted all-purpose flour

sifted confectioners' sugar

1. Put butter or margarine in a 2-1/2-quart mixing bowl and stir until fluffy.
2. Gradually blend in sugar and vanilla extract.
3. Add pecans and mix well.
4. Stir in flour, 1/4 cup at a time. This dough is stiff, but do not add liquid.
5. Shape dough into 1-inch balls and place them 1-1/2 inches apart on ungreased cooky sheets.
6. Bake in a preheated slow oven until cookies have browned lightly around the edges.
7. While still warm, roll cookies in confectioners' sugar.
8. Cool cookies on cooling racks and roll again in confectioners' sugar. Store in airtight containers.

Oven temperature: 325°F. (slow).

Baking time: 15 to 18 minutes.

Yield: 5 dozen cookies.

BUTTER-ALMOND BALLS

Replace pecans in the preceding recipe with 1 cup finely chopped blanched almonds.

Yield: 5 dozen.

CHOCOLATE-BIT PEANUT-BUTTER COOKIES

If peanut-butter cookies are your favorite, you will be sure to like these.

1 cup (2 sticks) butter or margarine, softened

3/4 cup chunky peanut butter

1/2 teaspoon soda

1/4 teaspoon salt

1-1/2 teaspoons vanilla extract

_____

1 cup granulated white sugar

1 cup light brown sugar, firmly packed and free from lumps

2 large eggs

2 cups sifted all-purpose flour

1 package (6 ounces) semisweet chocolate pieces (chocolate bits)

1. Put the first 5 ingredients in a 2-1/2-quart mixing bowl and mix until fluffy.
2. Gradually blend in both sugars, 1/2 cup at a time. Mix until well blended.
3. Beat in eggs, one at a time.
4. Stir in flour, 1/2 cup at a time.
5. Add the semisweet chocolate pieces and mix well.
6. Drop heaping one-half teaspoons of dough, 2 inches apart, onto greased cooky sheets.
7. With a metal spatula or teaspoon, flatten each cooky to about 1/4-inch thickness, keeping them round.
8. Bake in a preheated moderate oven until cookies have browned lightly around the edges. Cool on wire racks. Store in airtight containers.

Oven temperature: 350°F. (moderate).

Baking time: 8 to 9 minutes.

Yield: 7 dozen cookies.

PEANUT PEANUT-BUTTER COOKIES

Use the recipe for Chocolate-Bit Peanut-Butter Cookies, omitting the salt and chocolate bits and adding 1 cup chopped salted peanuts. Proceed according to recipe directions.
Yield: 7 dozen cookies.

CHRISTMAS CUT-OUT COOKIES

3 cups sifted all-purpose flour
2 teaspoons double-acting baking powder
___
1/2 teaspoon ground cloves
2 teaspoons ground cinnamon
2 teaspoons ground ginger
1 cup (2 sticks) butter or margarine, softened
___

1-1/2 cups sugar
1 large egg
pecans, raisins, colored granulated sugar, or Confectioners' Sugar and Water Icing (see following recipe)

1. Sift flour with baking powder and set aside.
2. Combine the next 4 ingredients and mix until fluffy.
3. Add 3/4 cup of the sugar, beat in egg, and add remaining 3/4 cup sugar. Mix well.
4. Stir in flour, about 1/2 cup at a time. This dough is stiff, but do not add liquid.
5. Refrigerate 3 to 4 hours or overnight or until the dough is stiff enough to roll.
6. Roll dough, about 1/3 at a time, to 1/8 inch thickness on a lightly floured flat surface.
7. Shape as desired with assorted cooky cutters, dipped in flour.

8. Place unbaked cookies on lightly greased cooky sheets.

9. If desired, decorate before baking with pecans, raisins, or colored granulated sugar. Or if desired, ice with Confectioners' Sugar and Water Icing after cookies have baked and cooled.

10. Bake until edges of cookies have browned lightly. Cool on wire racks. Store airtight.

Oven temperature: 375°F. (moderate).

Baking time: 8 to 10 minutes.

Yield: 5 dozen cookies, assorted sizes.

CONFECTIONERS' SUGAR AND WATER ICING

1 cup sifted confectioners' sugar

4 to 5 teaspoons water

1 to 2 drops food coloring (optional)

1. Combine confectioners' sugar with enough water to make mixture smooth and easy to spread.

2. Add food coloring (any color desired), if used.

Yield: 1/4 to 1/3 cup.

CRACKLE-TOP MOLASSES COOKIES

3/4 cup shortening

1 teaspoon soda

1/2 teaspoon salt

2 teaspoons ground ginger

1 teaspoon ground cinnamon

1 cup sugar

1/4 cup unsulphured molasses

1 large egg

2 cups sifted all-purpose flour

granulated sugar

1. Combine the first 5 ingredients in a 2-quart mixing bowl.
2. Gradually blend in the 1 cup sugar, mixing well after each addition.
3. Beat in molasses and egg.
4. Stir in flour, 1/2 cup at a time.
5. Chill the dough 2 to 3 hours or overnight or until the dough is stiff enough to handle.
6. Shape dough into 3/4-inch balls, dip the tops in granulated sugar, and place them on greased cooky sheets 1-1/2 inches apart to allow room for spreading.
7. Bake until the bottoms of the cookies have browned lightly. (If the cookies are baked too brown, they will have a bitter flavor.)
8. Cool cookies on wire racks. Store in airtight containers.

Oven temperature: 350°F. (moderate).
Baking time: 10 to 12 minutes.
Yield: About 3 dozen cookies.

COOKY BONBONS

1-1/2 cups (3 sticks) butter or margarine, softened
1/2 teaspoon salt
1 teaspoon almond extract
2 teaspoons vanilla extract

1-1/2 cups sifted confectioners' sugar

3 cups sifted all-purpose flour
filling (candied cherries, small pecans, small almonds, chocolate bits, and/or mixed candied fruit)

Almond-Vanilla Icing (see following recipe)

1. Put the first 4 ingredients in a 2-1/2-quart mixing bowl and mix until fluffy.

2. Gradually mix in sugar. Beat until fluffy.
3. Stir in flour, 1/3 cup at a time. This dough is stiff.
4. Roll about 1 teaspoon dough around 1 piece of filling. (a pecan, cherry, almond, chocolate bit, etc.)
5. Place 1 inch apart on ungreased cooky sheets.
6. Bake in a preheated slow oven until cookies have browned lightly on the bottoms. (Tops are not brown.)
7. Cool on wire racks. Ice with Almond-Vanilla Icing. Store in airtight containers.

Oven temperature: 325°F. (slow).
Baking time: 18 to 20 minutes.
Yield: 6 dozen bonbons.

ALMOND-VANILLA ICING

2 cups sifted confectioners' sugar
1/2 teaspoon almond extract
1 teaspoon vanilla extract
1/4 cup undiluted evaporated milk or light cream

1. Put all ingredients in a 1-quart mixing bowl. Mix well.

HOW TO ICE COOKY BONBONS

1. Divide icing into 4 equal parts in 4 small bowls.
2. Leave one part white and put 1 drop (green, pink, or yellow) food coloring in each of the remaining 3 parts.
3. Ice 5 to 6 bonbons at a time. Put them in a small bowl with 2 to 3 tablespoons icing. Stir with a fork until bonbons are well coated with icing.
4. Place a wire rack on a cooky sheet and with a fork transfer bonbons from the icing to the wire rack to dry. Scrape up all icing that has dripped onto the cooky sheet and re-use it.

CHOCOLATE BONBONS

1. Use the recipe for Cooky Bonbons.
2. Stir 2 squares (2 ounces) melted unsweetened chocolate into the fluffy butter or margarine and sugar mixture.
3. Proceed according to recipe directions, adding 2 to 3 tablespoons milk or light cream if the dough tends to be too stiff.
4. Ice, when cold, with Chocolate Icing (see following recipe) and colored Almond-Vanilla icing.

CHOCOLATE ICING

1 cup sifted confectioners' sugar

1/4 cup undiluted evaporated milk or light cream

1/4 teaspoon almond extract

1/2 teaspoon vanilla extract

1 square (1 ounce) unsweetened chocolate, melted

1. Combine all ingredients in a 1-quart mixing bowl.
2. Proceed according to directions, How to Ice Cooky Bonbons.
Yield: Sufficient icing for 3 dozen bonbons.

DATE AND NUT FUDGE SQUARES

2/3 cup sifted all-purpose flour

1/4 teaspoon salt

1/8 teaspoon soda

6 tablespoons butter or margarine

2 squares (2 ounces) unsweetened chocolate

1 cup dark brown sugar, firmly packed

1-1/2 teaspoons vanilla extract

2 large eggs

2 tablespoons milk

3/4 cup finely chopped dates

3/4 cup chopped pecans or walnuts

1. Sift flour again with salt and soda. Set aside.
2. In the top of a 1-1/2-quart double boiler, melt butter or margarine and chocolate over hot water.
3. Add sugar and vanilla extract. Mix well.
4. Beat in eggs, one at a time.
5. Stir in flour mixture and milk.
6. Fold in dates and pecans or walnuts until blended.
7. Spread the batter over the bottom of a well-greased, lightly floured 9 x 9 x 2-inch pan.
8. Bake in a preheated moderate oven until firm in the center.
9. Turn out onto a wire rack to cool.
10. Cut into 32 squares. Store airtight.

Oven temperature: 350°F. (moderate).

Baking time: 45 minutes.

Yield: 32 squares.

JUMBO SOFT CHOCOLATE COOKIES

2 cups light brown sugar, firmly packed

1 cup shortening
_____

1 teaspoon salt

1 teaspoon soda

2 teaspoons vanilla extract

3 squares (3 ounces) unsweetened chocolate, melted
_____

2 large eggs

2-1/2 cups sifted all-purpose flour

1 cup sour milk or buttermilk

1 cup chopped pecans or walnuts

1. Press out all lumps in the brown sugar, and gradually blend it with shortening.

2. Stir in the next 4 ingredients.
3. Beat in eggs, one at a time.
4. Add flour alternately with sour milk or buttermilk.
5. Stir in pecans or walnuts.
6. Chill dough 1 to 2 hours or until stiffened slightly.
7. Drop rounded tablespoons of dough 2 inches apart onto lightly greased cooky sheets to allow room for spreading.
8. Bake until cookies have browned lightly around the edges.
9. Transfer cookies to wire cooling racks. Store airtight when cold.

Oven temperature: 375°F. (moderate).
Baking time: 15 to 18 minutes.
Yield: 2-1/2 dozen 3-inch cookies.

OLD-FASHIONED DROPPED SUGAR COOKIES

3 cups sifted all-purpose flour
1 teaspoon double-acting baking powder
1/2 teaspoon salt

1-1/2 cups sugar
2 teaspoons vanilla extract
2 large eggs
2 tablespoons milk

1 cup (2 sticks) butter or margarine, softened

1. Sift the first 3 ingredients together and set aside.
2. Put butter or margarine in a 2-quart mixing bowl and gradually blend in sugar, 1/4 cup at a time.
3. Beat in vanilla extract and eggs.
4. Stir in milk and gradually add flour mixture, 1/3 cup at a time.

5. Drop heaping teaspoons of dough 2 inches apart onto greased cooky sheets.
6. Bake in a preheated moderate oven until cookies have browned lightly around the edges.
7. Cool on wire racks. Store airtight.

Oven temperature: 375°F. (moderate).

Baking time: 15 minutes.

Yield: 3 dozen cookies, 2-1/2 inches diameter.

REFRIGERATOR COOKIES

2-1/4 cups sifted all-purpose flour

3/4 teaspoon double-acting baking powder

1/4 teaspoon salt

1 cup sugar

3/4 cup shortening

1-1/2 teaspoons vanilla extract

1/2 cup chopped pecans or walnuts (optional)

1 large egg

1. Sift the first 3 ingredients together and set aside.
2. Blend sugar with shortening and vanilla extract.
3. Stir in pecans or walnuts, if used.
4. Beat in egg.
5. Stir in flour mixture, 1/2 cup at a time. Mix well.
6. Divide the dough in half, place on waxed paper, and shape each half into a roll 1-1/2 inches in diameter.
7. Wrap the rolls in waxed paper or foil.
8. Refrigerate several hours or overnight, or for several days.
9. When ready to bake, cut rolls into slices 1/8 inch thick.

Place slices about 1 inch apart on lightly greased cooky sheets.

10. Bake in a preheated moderate oven until cookies have browned lightly around the edges.
11. Cool on cooling racks. Store in airtight containers.

Oven temperature: 375°F. (moderate).

Baking time: 5 to 6 minutes.

Yield: Approximately 6 dozen cookies.

VARIATIONS

ORANGE REFRIGERATOR COOKIES

Use the recipe for Refrigerator Cookies, and blend 1 tablespoon grated orange rind and 1/2 teaspoon grated lemon rind with the sugar and shortening mixture. Proceed according to the recipe directions.

RIBBON REFRIGERATOR COOKIES

1. Remove 1 side from a cardboard 1-quart milk carton, leaving the remaining 3 sides and 2 ends intact. Rinse the carton with cold water and wipe it dry. Set aside.
2. Make the preceding recipe for Refrigerator Cookies, omitting the nuts, and divide the dough into 3 parts.
3. Pat 1 part of the dough evenly over the bottom of the milk carton.
4. Blend 1 square (1 ounce) melted chocolate with 1 of the remaining parts of the dough, put it in the milk carton and pat it evenly over the plain layer of dough.

5. Mix 8 drops of red or green food coloring with remaining dough and pat it evenly over the chocolate layer.
6. Wrap the carton in foil. Chill several hours, overnight, or for several days.
7. When ready to bake the cookies, tear the sides from milk carton and place the dough on a board.
8. Cut the dough into slices 1/8 inch thick and bake according to the directions in the recipe.

Yield: 3 dozen cookies.

SPICE CRISPIES

1 teaspoon soda
1/2 teaspoon salt
1 teaspoon ground cinnamon
1-1/2 teaspoons ground ginger
1/2 cup shortening
1/4 cup white granulated sugar

1/2 cup light or dark brown sugar, firmly packed
1 large egg
1/2 cup unsulphured molasses mixed with 1-1/2 teaspoons cider vinegar
2-1/2 cups sifted all-purpose flour

1. Combine first 5 ingredients in a 2-quart mixing bowl.
2. Gradually blend in white sugar and brown sugar.
3. Beat in egg.
4. Stir in molasses and vinegar mixture.
5. Add 1/2 cup flour at a time, mixing well after each addition.
6. Drop heaping 1/2 teaspoons of dough, 2 inches apart onto greased cooky sheets.

7. Flatten dough to 1/8 inch thickness with the bottom of a glass covered with a damp-wet cloth.
8. Bake until cookies have browned lightly around the edges. (Do not bake cookies too brown.)
9. Cool on wire racks. Store in airtight containers.

Oven temperature: 400°F. (hot).

Baking time: 6 to 8 minutes.

Yield: 5 dozen cookies.

SYMBOL COOKIES

(CHANUKAH)

You will like these cookies whether or not you are observing the Jewish holiday Chanukah.

2 cups sifted all-purpose flour
1/2 teaspoon salt
2 teaspoons double-acting baking powder
1 cup sugar
1/2 cup vegetable shortening
1 teaspoon vanilla extract
1 large egg
2 tablespoons orange juice
Confectioners' Sugar and Water Icing (optional)

1. Sift together the first 3 ingredients and set aside.
2. Gradually blend sugar with shortening and vanilla extract.
3. Beat in egg. Stir in orange juice.
4. Stir in flour mixture, about 1/2 cup at a time.
5. Chill dough 2 to 3 hours or overnight or until dough is stiff enough to roll.

6. Roll dough to 1/8 inch thickness on a lightly floured surface.

7. Cut dough into symbol shapes with Chanukah cooky cutters or with cardboard patterns, or cut round cookies with a round cooky cutter and make Chanukah symbols on them with Confectioners' Sugar and Water Icing.

8. Bake on ungreased cooky sheets until cookies have browned lightly around the edges.

9. Transfer cookies to a wire cooling rack. Cool. When cooled, store in airtight containers.

10. Frost as desired with Confectioners' Sugar and Water Icing.

Oven temperature: 375°F. (moderate).

Baking time: 8 to 10 minutes.

Yield: 5 dozen 2-1/2-inch round cookies.

VANILLA WAFERS

2 cups sifted all-purpose flour
2 teaspoons double-acting
  baking powder
1/2 teaspoon salt
1-1/2 teaspoons vanilla extract

2/3 cup (1-1/4 sticks) butter
  or margarine, softened
1 cup sugar
1 large egg
1/4 cup milk

1. Sift together the first 3 ingredients and set aside.
2. Add vanilla extract to butter (or margarine) and mix well.
3. Gradually blend in sugar. Beat in egg.
4. Add sifted flour mixture alternately with milk.

5. Drop rounded 1/2 teaspoons of dough onto ungreased cooky sheets 2 inches apart to allow room for spreading.
6. Flatten cookies to 1/16 inch thickness with a glass covered with a wet-damp cloth.
7. Bake until cookies have browned lightly around the edges. Transfer cookies to cooling racks. Store airtight when cold.

Oven temperature: (375°F.), moderate.

Baking time: 10 to 12 minutes.

Yield: 4-1/2 dozen cookies.

WHOLE-WHEAT COOKIES

1 cup sugar

3 cups unsifted whole-wheat flour

1/2 teaspoon salt

2 teaspoons soda

2 teaspoons ground cinnamon

1 teaspoon ground ginger

3/4 cup shortening

1 large egg, beaten

3/4 cup unsulphured molasses

1 tablespoon lemon juice or cider vinegar

1. Put the first 6 ingredients in a 2-1/2-quart mixing bowl and mix well.
2. Add shortening and cut it in with a pastry blender or with the fingers until the mixture resembles fine crumbs.
3. Combine egg, molasses, and lemon juice or vinegar and add to crumb mixture. Mix well. Chill dough if it is too soft to handle.
4. Shape dough into 3/4-inch balls and place them 2 inches apart on greased cooky sheets, to allow room for spreading.
5. Flatten the cookies with the tines of a fork.

6. Bake in a preheated moderate oven until the cookies have browned lightly around the edges.

7. Cool on wire cooling racks. Store in airtight containers.

Oven temperature: 375°F. (moderate).

Baking time: about 10 minutes.

Yield: About 7 dozen cookies.

DESSERTS

Desserts vary considerably. Some are light and are appropriate for ending a heavy meal, while others are heavy and should be served after a light meal. Custards, puddings, pies, and fruit desserts are included in this chapter.

APPLESAUCE PUDDING

1-1/2 cups fine dry bread-crumbs

1/8 teaspoon salt

1/2 teaspoon ground nutmeg

1/2 cup light brown sugar, firmly packed

1/2 cup (1 stick) butter or margarine, melted

1 can (17 ounces) applesauce or 2 cups homemade apple-sauce

1/3 cup heavy cream, whipped (optional)

2 teaspoons sugar (optional)

1. Combine the first 3 ingredients with 1/4 cup of the brown sugar.
2. Add melted butter or margarine and mix well.

3. Pat one-half the crumb mixture over the bottom of a buttered 10 x 6 x 2-inch baking dish. Bake 10 minutes in a preheated moderate oven.
4. Mix remaining 1/4 cup brown sugar with applesauce. Spread mixture over the baked crumbs.
5. Sprinkle remaining crumb mixture over the top. Bake 20 minutes or until crumbs have browned.
6. Serve plain or with whipped cream sweetened with 2 teaspoons sugar.

Oven temperature: 375°F. (moderate).

Total baking time: 30 minutes.

Yield: 6 servings.

BAKED APPLES AND RHUBARB

3 cups (3 to 4 medium-large) diced, pared apples

4 cups (1-1/2 pounds) diced fresh or frozen rhubarb*

about 1 cup sugar

1/4 teaspoon salt

3 sticks cinnamon, each 2 inches long

1. Put the first 4 ingredients in a 2-quart casserole. Mix well.
2. Bury cinnamon sticks in the center of the fruit.
3. Cover and bake until apples and rhubarb are soft.
4. Remove and discard cinnamon sticks and stir the mixture well. Add more sugar if desired.
5. Serve as dessert, warm or chilled, in fruit dishes.

Oven temperature: 375°F. (moderate).

Baking time: 1-1/4 hours. *If frozen rhubarb is used increase the baking time to 1-1/2 hours.

Yield: 8 servings.

BAKED CUSTARD
(Made with sweetened condensed milk)

3 large eggs, beaten
1 can (14 ounces) sweetened condensed milk
1/4 teaspoon salt

1-1/2 teaspoons vanilla extract

2-1/4 cups hot water
ground nutmeg

1. Put the first 4 ingredients in a 2-quart mixing bowl and mix well.
2. Gradually stir in the hot water.
3. Pour the mixture into 7 6-ounce custard cups and sprinkle with ground nutmeg.
4. Place the cups in a pan of hot water.
5. Bake in a preheated slow oven until a knife inserted in the center comes out clean.

Oven temperature: 325°F. (slow).
Baking time: 1 hour.
Yield: 7 servings.

BAKED RICE CUSTARD

A good economical dessert to make when you have leftover rice, and when the oven is in use for baking another dish at the same temperature.

2 large egg yolks
1 large whole egg

1/3 cup sugar
1/16 teaspoon salt
1/8 teaspoon ground nutmeg or ground mace

3/4 teaspoon vanilla extract
1/2 cup leftover cooked rice

1-1/4 cups milk, heated
Meringue (see following recipe)

1. Put egg yolks and whole egg in a 2-quart mixing bowl and beat until the eggs are blended.
2. Stir in the next 5 ingredients.
3. Add the milk and mix well.
4. Pour the mixture into a buttered 1-quart casserole.
5. Place the casserole in a pan of hot water.
6. Bake in a preheated slow oven until the custard is soft-firm in the center.
7. Remove the custard from the oven and spread the Meringue over the top.
8. Bake at the same temperature until the Meringue has browned lightly. Serve warm or cold.

Oven temperature: 325°F. (slow).

Baking time: For custard, 30 minutes; for meringue, 15 minutes.

Yield: 4 servings.

MERINGUE

2 large egg whites   3 tablespoons sugar
dash of salt

1. Put egg whites and salt in a 2-quart mixing bowl and beat them until they stand in soft, stiff peaks.
2. Gradually beat in the sugar, 1/2 tablespoon at a time.
3. Continue beating until mixture stands in stiff peaks.
4. Spread the meringue over the Baked Rice Custard. Bake as directed in the recipe for Baked Rice Custard.

Yield: Meringue sufficient to cover a 4-serving custard or pudding.

Note: For a Meringue made with 3 egg whites, increase the sugar to 5 tablespoons, and proceed following the directions for making Merinque.

BANANA REFRIGERATOR CAKE

30 chocolate wafers or ginger wafers
1 cup heavy cream
1 tablespoon sugar

1/2 teaspoon vanilla extract
1 cup sliced bananas
1/2 square unsweetened chocolate, shaved

1. Arrange 15 of the wafers, overlapping, over the bottom of a 7-inch springform pan (cheesecake pan).
2. Beat cream with sugar and vanilla extract until it stands in soft, stiff peaks.
3. Spread half the whipped cream over the wafers.
4. Arrange all the bananas over the cream.
5. Top the bananas with remaining 15 wafers and whipped cream, in the order given.
6. Refrigerate until ready to serve. Garnish the top with shaved unsweetened chocolate.
7. Serve in pie-shaped wedges.
Yield: 6 servings.

BUSY-DAY APPLE MOUSSE

2 cups (16-ounce can) sweetened applesauce
1 teaspoon vanilla extract

1 cup heavy cream, whipped
1/2 square (1/2 ounce) unsweetened chocolate, grated

1. Combine applesauce and vanilla extract.
2. Fold in whipped cream and spoon into sherbet glasses.
3. Chill at least 1 hour.
4. Just before serving, sprinkle the tops with grated chocolate.
Yield: 6 servings.

CANTALOUPE COUPE

1 medium-sized ripe cantaloupe

2 tablespoons Kirsch
1 pint vanilla ice cream

1. Cut cantaloupe in half, remove the seeds, and drain well.
2. With a French melon-ball cutter or a half teaspoon measure cut the cantaloupe into balls, or cut the melon into dice.
3. Add the Kirsch and marinate the melon 3 to 4 hours.
4. Fill sherbet glasses with alternating layers of cantaloupe and ice cream, having the cantaloupe on the bottom and top.
Yield: 6 servings.

CANTALOUPE AND STRAWBERRY CUP

2 cups sliced fresh strawberries
1/2 cup sugar

3 cups cantaloupe balls or
diced cantaloupe
fresh mint

1. Combine strawberries and sugar and chill 1 or more hours.
2. Shortly before serving, put the strawberries through a sieve and mix with the cantaloupe balls.

3. Serve in sherbet glasses, garnish with sprigs of fresh mint.
Yield: 6 servings.

COCONUT CUSTARD PUDDING

2 cups milk
1/4 cup sugar
1/4 teaspoon salt
1-1/2 teaspoons vanilla extract

3 large eggs, lightly beaten
3/4 cup moist flaked coconut
ground nutmeg

1. Combine 1/4 cup of the milk with next 4 ingredients.
2. Heat remaining 1-3/4 cups milk only until hot, and gradually add to the egg mixture.
3. Stir in coconut.
4. Pour the mixture into a buttered 1-quart casserole.
5. Sprinkle nutmeg on top.
6. Place the casserole in a pan of hot water.
7. Bake until a knife inserted in the center comes out clean.
Oven temperature: 300°F. (slow).
Baking time: 1 hour.
Yield: 6 servings.

CHANTILLY PEACH PARFAIT

1 pint vanilla ice cream
1-1/2 cups heavy cream
3/4 cup Toasted Slivered Almonds

4 to 5 medium-sized ripe peaches, peeled and sliced
1 tablespoon sugar

1. Remove ice cream from freezer and let stand at room temperature until soft but not melted, about 30 minutes.
2. Whip 1 cup of the cream and fold it into the ice cream along with 1/2 cup of the Toasted Slivered Almonds.
3. Turn the mixture into ice cube trays or into an 8 x 8 x 2-inch pan and freeze until almost firm.
4. Fill parfait glasses with alternating layers of ice cream and sliced peaches.
5. Let the parfait-filled glasses stand in the freezer until ready to serve.
6. Just before serving, whip the remaining 1/2 cup heavy cream with the sugar and put a dollop on each serving. Sprinkle with the remaining Toasted Slivered Almonds. Serve at once.

Makes 6 to 8 servings.

CHOCOLATE POTS DE CRÈME

1/2 cup sugar
6 large egg yolks, beaten until
   light and lemon colored

1/4 cup cold light cream
1/8 teaspoon salt

1-1/2 teaspoons vanilla extract

2 squares (2 ounces) unsweetened chocolate, melted
1-3/4 cups light cream, heated
Chantilly Crème (see following recipe)

1. Gradually beat sugar into beaten egg yolks.
2. Stir in the next 3 ingredients.
3. Blend chocolate with hot cream, and add it to the egg mixture. Mix well.

4. Strain the mixture through a fine sieve into 6 custard cups (6 ounces each).
5. Place the cups in a pan of hot water.
6. Cover and bake in a preheated slow oven until a knife inserted in the center comes out clean.
7. Serve cold, garnished with Chantilly Crème.

Oven temperature: 325°F. (slow).

Baking time: Approximately 55 minutes.

Yield: 6 servings.

CHANTILLY CRÈME

1 tablespoon sifted confectioners' sugar

1/4 teaspoon vanilla extract
1/2 cup heavy cream

1. Put all ingredients in a small mixing bowl and beat with an electric beater or rotary beater until cream stands in soft, stiff peaks.
2. Serve as a topping for desserts and fruits.

Yield: Approximately 1 cup.

COFFEE CREAM

1 envelope unflavored gelatin
1/2 cup sugar
1-1/2 teaspoons instant coffee
1/16 teaspoon salt
3/4 cup milk

1 teaspoon vanilla extract
1 cup heavy cream, whipped
chopped pecans, chocolate decorettes, or shaved unsweetened chocolate

1. Combine the first 5 ingredients in a 1-quart saucepan. Let mixture stand 5 minutes to soften gelatin.

2. Heat the mixture *only* until it is hot. (Do not boil.)
3. Place saucepan in a bowl of ice water to chill the mixture until it is about as thick as fresh egg whites.
4. Add vanilla extract and gently fold the mixture into the whipped cream.
5. Spoon the cream into sherbet glasses. Chill until ready to serve, 3 to 4 hours or overnight.
6. Garnish with chopped pecans, chocolate decorettes, or shaved unsweetened chocolate.

Yield: 6 servings.

CREAMY PINEAPPLE SQUARES

An easy dessert to make for the bridge club. It never fails.

1/2 cup milk
1/8 teaspoon salt
24 regular size marshmallows
_____
1 cup heavy cream, whipped
1/2 teaspoon ground nutmeg

1/4 teaspoon grated lemon rind
_____
1/4 cup graham cracker crumbs
1 cup (8-ounce can) crushed pineapple, well drained

1. Put the first 3 ingredients in the top of a 2-quart double boiler, place over hot water, and heat until the marshmallows have melted.
2. Cool the mixture until it begins to thicken.
3. Fold in the next 3 ingredients.
4. Sprinkle 2 tablespoons of the graham cracker crumbs over the bottom of a buttered 9 x 9 x 2-inch pan.

5. Pour 1/2 the marshmallow mixture into the crumbed, buttered pan and cover with 1/2 cup of the crushed pineapple.
6. Repeat, using remaining marshmallow mixture and crushed pineapple.
7. Sprinkle the top with remaining 2 tablespoons graham cracker crumbs.
8. Refrigerate several hours, or overnight, or until ready to serve.
9. Cut into squares and serve on dessert plates. If desired, garnish with additional whipped cream sweetened to taste.

Yield: 8 servings.

FLAN

1 cup sugar
1/4 cup hot water

4 large eggs, lightly beaten
1/4 teaspoon salt

1 teaspoon vanilla extract

1 cup light cream
1 cup milk
whipped cream (optional)

1. Put 1/2 cup of the sugar in a 3-cup saucepan.
2. Stir and cook over medium heat until sugar has melted and is golden.
3. Gradually pour in hot water. (The syrup will lump at this stage, but this is as it should be.)
4. Boil the mixture until all lumps have melted.
5. Put 1 tablespoon of the syrup in each of six 6-ounce custard cups and set aside until syrup hardens.
6. Combine remaining 1/2 cup sugar with the next 3 ingredients and 1/4 cup of the cream. Mix well.

7. Heat remaining 3/4 cup cream and milk and gradually stir into the egg mixture.
8. Pour an equal amount of the mixture into each of the custard cups, filling to within 1/2 inch of the top.
9. Place cups in a pan of hot water. Bake until a knife inserted in the center of the custard comes out clean.
10. Serve cold, with whipped cream if desired.

Oven temperature: 325°F. (slow).

Baking time: 45 to 50 minutes.

Yield: 6 servings.

GINGER CREAM

1 envelope unflavored gelatin
1/4 cup cold water

1/4 cup sugar
1/16 teaspoon salt
1 large egg, beaten lightly

1 cup milk

3 tablespoons syrup from preserved ginger

1 teaspoon vanilla extract

1/4 cup chopped preserved ginger

1 cup heavy cream, whipped

1. Mix gelatin with water and let stand until ready to use.
2. Put the next 3 ingredients in the top of a 1-quart double boiler. Mix well.
3. Stir in milk and cook, stirring frequently, over hot water (not boiling) until the custard coats a metal spoon, 8 to 10 minutes.
4. Remove custard from heat and stir in softened gelatin. Stir until gelatin is dissolved.

5. Place pan in a bowl of ice water to chill until custard is cold and begins to set.
6. Stir in the next 3 ingredients and gently fold the custard into the whipped cream.
7. Spoon the cream into sherbet glasses. Chill until ready to serve, 3 to 4 hours or overnight.
8. Garnish each with a piece of preserved ginger or a candied cherry.

Yield: 6 servings.

GINGERED BLUEBERRY COMPOTE

2 cups (1-pint basket) raw blueberries, washed and drained
1 cup orange juice
1 tablespoon lemon juice
3 tablespoons sugar
2 tablespoons minced preserved ginger
fresh mint leaves if available

1. Combine the first 4 ingredients and chill 1 to 2 hours. Add ginger.
2. Serve in compotes or fruit dishes, and garnish with fresh mint leaves, if available.

Yield: 6 servings.

LEMON CREAM

1 package (4 ounces) lemon pudding mix
1/16 teaspoon salt
2 large egg whites
3 tablespoons sugar
1 teaspoon vanilla extract
1-1/4 cups heavy cream
shaved unsweetened chocolate or toasted coconut (optional)

1. Make pudding according to package directions, and cool.
2. Add salt to egg whites and beat until they stand in soft, stiff peaks.
3. Gradually beat sugar and vanilla extract into the beaten egg whites and set them aside.
4. Whip 1 cup of the cream until it stands in peaks and fold it into the lemon cream along with beaten egg whites.
5. Spoon lemon cream into sherbet glasses. Chill.
6. Just before serving, garnish with remaining 1/4 cup heavy cream whipped until stiff. If desired sprinkle shaved unsweetened chocolate or toasted coconut over the cream.

Yield: 6 servings.

MELON BALLS IN MINT SAUCE

4 cups fresh cantaloupe balls or honeydew-melon balls
2/3 cup sugar
1/3 cup lemon juice

2 tablespoons finely chopped mint

sprigs of fresh mint

1. Combine the first 4 ingredients, mix lightly but well, and chill 3 to 4 hours or overnight.
2. Serve in sherbet glasses. Garnish with sprigs of fresh mint.

Yield: 6 servings.

MINTED AMBROSIA

navel oranges, peeled and cut into sections

mint syrup or crème de menthe
flaked coconut

1. Put orange sections in sherbet glasses, using about 1-1/2 medium-sized navel oranges for each glass.
2. Pour 1 tablespoon mint syrup or crème de menthe over each serving and sprinkle with flaked coconut.

ORANGE AND SHERBET CUP

6 medium-sized navel oranges, peeled and cut into sections

6 tablespoons Cointreau (or Triple Sec optional)

6 scoops lemon ice or lime ice (or sherbet)

1. Put orange sections in sherbet glasses, using 1 orange for each serving.
2. Sprinkle 1 tablespoon Cointreau or Triple Sec over each serving, if desired, and place 1 scoop of lemon ice or lime ice (or sherbet) over each serving.
3. Serve for the first course or for dessert.

Yield: 6 servings.

PEACH MELBA

6 large canned peach halves packed in heavy syrup

6 scoops vanilla ice cream

1 cup frozen sweetened raspberries, defrosted

1. Place a peach half in each of 6 dessert dishes, and top each with a scoop of vanilla ice cream.
2. Spoon about 2-1/2 tablespoons defrosted raspberries over the ice cream. Serve promptly.

Yield: 6 servings.

BLUEBERRY MELBA

In the recipe for Peach Melba, replace each peach half with 1/3 cup fresh blueberries. Top with vanilla ice cream and defrosted frozen raspberries according to directions in the recipe. Yield: 6 servings.

PEACH PANDOWDY

6 cups (about 3 pounds) peeled, sliced, raw peaches
1 cup sugar
1/4 teaspoon salt

3 tablespoons butter or margarine

1-1/2 cups sifted all-purpose flour

3/4 teaspoon salt
3 teaspoons double-acting baking powder
2 tablespoons sugar

1/3 cup shortening
1 large egg, beaten
1/2 cup milk

1. Combine the first 3 ingredients and turn the mixture into a 9 x 9 x 2-inch baking dish.
2. Dot with butter or margarine and set aside.
3. Sift the next 4 ingredients together into a 1-1/2-quart mixing bowl.
4. Add shortening. With a pastry blender or 2 knives, cut shortening in until mixture resembles medium-fine crumbs.
5. Mix the beaten egg with the milk and stir into the flour mixture to form a drop batter.
6. Drop the batter in 8 mounds over the top of the peaches.

7. Bake uncovered, in a preheated hot oven for 30 minutes. Cover dish with foil and bake 10 minutes more. Serve warm.

Oven temperature: 425°F. (hot).

Baking time: 40 minutes.

Yield: 8 servings.

PINEAPPLE REFRIGERATOR CAKE

If you are not counting calories, this dessert is perfect to serve at the end of a light meal.

3 tablespoons cornstarch

1/4 teaspoon salt

3/4 cup canned pineapple juice

4-1/2 cups sifted confectioners' sugar

1/2 teaspoon grated lemon rind

3/4 cup (1-1/2 sticks) butter or margarine

2 layers sponge cake, 8 inches diameter

1 package ladyfingers, split

1 cup well-drained crushed pineapple

1/2 cup heavy cream, whipped

1. Combine the first 3 ingredients in a small saucepan.
2. Stir and cook over moderate heat until the mixture is very thick.
3. Remove the saucepan from the heat and stir in 1/2 cup of the confectioners' sugar.
4. Add remaining 4 cups confectioners' sugar alternately with butter or margarine and lemon rind. Cool.
5. Split each cake layer, making 4 thin layers.

6. Place 1 cake layer, cut side up, in an 8-1/2-inch spring-form pan (cheesecake pan).
7. Stand lady fingers around the sides of the pan, between the cake layer and sides of the pan.
8. Spread cake layer with 1/4 of the cooked mixture. Then spread with 1/3 cup drained crushed pineapple.
9. Repeat this procedure, using the remaining cake, cooked mixture, and crushed pineapple. Chill 10 to 12 hours.
10. Shortly before serving, remove sides of pan from the cake, and place the cake on a cake plate. Spread whipped cream over the top. To serve, cut cake into wedges.

Yield: 10 to 12 servings.

FRESH STRAWBERRIES IN CHANTILLY CRÈME

1 quart fresh strawberries
3 tablespoons sugar
___
1 cup heavy cream
2 tablespoons sifted confectioners' sugar

1/2 teaspoon vanilla extract
___
1 to 2 tablespoons Cointreau or Kirsch (optional)

1. Pick out 6 of the prettiest strawberries, leave caps attached and set aside to use as a garnish.
2. Wash remaining strawberries and remove caps.
3. Slice strawberries and sprinkle with the 3 tablespoons sugar. Set aside.
4. Put the next 3 ingredients in a 1-quart mixing bowl and beat *only* until the cream stands in soft peaks when the beater is withdrawn.

5. Fold in the sliced strawberries and Kirsch or Cointreau, if used.
6. Turn mixture into an ice-cube tray and let stand in the freezer about 20 minutes or until chilled. *Do not freeze.*
7. Serve in sherbet glasses and top each with a washed, whole, uncapped strawberry. Serve at once.

Yield: 6 servings.

STRAWBERRY TRIFLE

Bring this attractive dessert to the table in the pretty glass bowl in which it was made, and serve it in your best dessert plates.

1 quart firm ripe strawberries
1/2 cup sugar
2 round 8-inch sponge cake layers

2-1/2 cups Soft Custard
1/2 cup heavy cream, whipped and sweetened with 1 tablespoon sugar

1. Wash strawberries. Select 8 of the prettiest ones and place them, caps attached, in a jar. Cover and refrigerate for use as a garnish.
2. Remove caps from remaining strawberries, slice, add sugar, and refrigerate 30 minutes.
3. Put one cake layer in your prettiest 2-quart glass bowl, which should measure 9 or 10 inches across the bottom.
4. Distribute half the sugared berries over the cake layer and pour 1 cup of the Soft Custard over all.
5. Top with second sponge cake layer.

6. Cover with remaining berries and pour remaining 1-1/2 cups custard over the berries.
7. Cover the bowl and refrigerate 10 to 12 hours or overnight.
8. Shortly before serving, spread sweetened whipped cream over the top.
9. Garnish with the 8 whole strawberries.

Yield: 8 servings.

SOFT CUSTARD

1/4 cup sugar
1/4 teaspoon salt
2 large eggs, beaten lightly
_____
1-1/2 cups milk

1 teaspoon vanilla extract
1/4 teaspoon ground nutmeg
  (optional)

1. Put the first 3 ingredients in a 1-quart saucepan or in the top of a 1-quart double boiler.
2. Stir in 1/4 cup of the milk.
3. Heat remaining milk *only* until hot, and add to the egg and sugar mixture; mix well.
4. Cook, stirring frequently, over low heat or hot water until the custard coats a metal spoon.
5. Remove custard from heat and cool.
6. Stir in vanilla extract and nutmeg, if used.
7. Serve in sherbet glasses, or over fruit or plain cake.

Yield: About 1-1/2 cups.

WATERMELON FRUIT JELLY

2 envelopes unflavored gelatin
1/2 cup water
4 cups diced watermelon
2 tablespoons lemon juice or lime juice
1/4 cup sugar
1/8 teaspoon salt
1/3 cup blueberries
1/2 cup diced oranges
1 cup green seedless grapes
1/3 cup heavy cream, whipped (optional)

1. In a custard cup or teacup, mix gelatin and water and let it stand 5 minutes to soften.
2. Place cup in a pan of hot water and let stand 3 to 4 minutes to melt gelatin. Set aside, keeping the cup in the hot water until ready to use.
3. Put watermelon through a fine sieve and measure juice. (There should be 2 cups.)
4. Mix watermelon juice with melted gelatin and the next 3 ingredients in a mixing bowl. Stir until sugar has dissolved.
5. Place the bowl in a pan of ice water or in the freezer until mixture begins to thicken, about as thick as fresh egg whites.
6. Fold in blueberries, oranges, and grapes.
7. Refrigerate until the mixture is firm and you are ready to serve it.
8. Serve in sherbet glasses, topped with whipped cream if desired.

Yield: 4-1/2 cups or 8 servings.

EASY-TO-MAKE PLUM PUDDING

Molasses and spice and everything nice is what this pudding is made of. It is easy on the budget and light on kitchen labor. Steam it in 2 1-quart pudding molds or in 2 1-pound coffee cans, with foil tied tightly over the tops.

2 cups sifted all-purpose flour
1/4 cup sugar
1 teaspoon soda
1 teaspoon salt
1/2 teaspoon ground cloves
1-1/2 teaspoons ground cinnamon
_____
2 large eggs, beaten
3/4 cup unsulphured molasses

1/3 cup (3/4 stick) butter or margarine, melted
_____
1 cup diced or sliced citron
2 cups chopped, pitted, dried dates
2 cups seedless raisins
1/4 cup milk, apple cider, or pineapple juice
hard sauce, Foamy Sauce, or whipped cream

1. Sift the first 6 ingredients together into a large mixing bowl.
2. Add eggs, molasses, and butter or margarine. Mix well.
3. Stir in remaining ingredients.
4. Grease 2 1-quart pudding molds or 2 1-pound coffee cans well and sprinkle them with granulated sugar.
5. Fill molds or cans 2/3 full with the pudding mixture.
6. Cover molds or cans with foil and place them on trivets or racks in a deep kettle.
7. Pour in enough boiling water to come half way up the sides of the molds.

8. Cover the kettle and steam the puddings 3 hours, or until a cake tester inserted in the center comes out clean. (Start counting the time when the water in the kettle begins to boil.)

9. This pudding may be made several weeks before it is served and soaked in brandy, rum, or wine during this aging period.

10. Reheat the puddings in the molds with covers on in a kettle of boiling water, about 1 hour before serving.

11. Serve with hard sauce, Foamy Sauce or whipped cream flavored with brandy, rum, or grated orange and lemon rind.

Yield: 2 1-quart molds, or about 16 servings.

HOW TO BLANCH, TOAST, AND SAUTÉ ALMONDS

BLANCHED ALMONDS

1. Put almonds in a small saucepan, cover with cold water, and bring to boiling point. (Do not boil.)
2. Remove almonds from heat at once and drain off water.
3. Slip off the skins by pressing almonds between forefinger and thumb.
4. Put blanched almonds on paper towels and pat them dry.

TOASTED ALMONDS

1. Put blanched almonds in a baking pan, allowing 1 tablespoon salad oil or melted butter to 1 cup almonds. Mix well to coat almonds lightly with oil or butter.

2. Toast in a preheated slow oven (300°F.) 20 to 25 minutes or until the almonds are golden.
3. If almonds are to be used slivered, cut blanched almonds into lengthwise strips (slivers) before toasting. Reduce the toasting time to about 15 minutes.

SAUTÉED ALMONDS

1. Heat salad oil or butter (2 tablespoons oil or butter to 1 cup blanched almonds) in a skillet or saucepan.
2. Add blanched almonds and cook, stirring, about 1 minute or until the almonds are golden.

FISH AND SHELLFISH

Fish and shellfish are available in fresh, quick-frozen, and canned forms. Fish is also available salted, smoked, and pickled. When buying fresh fish or shellfish, be sure that it has a good fresh color and odor, and that the flesh of fish is firm, not soft.

CRUSTY BAKED FISH

2 halibut steaks or 2 swordfish steaks, about 1 pound each, cut 1/2 inch thick
2 teaspoons salt
1/2 cup milk
1 cup slightly crushed corn flakes
6 tablespoons butter or margarine, melted
Tartare Sauce

1. Cut fish steaks into 6 serving pieces.
2. Add salt to milk, dip the fish into the mixture, and then into the cornflakes.
3. Arrange fish in a buttered shallow baking pan. Spoon 1 tablespoon melted butter or margarine over each serving.

4. Bake in a preheated hot oven until fish flakes when tested with a fork and cornflakes are crusty brown.
5. Serve with Tartare Sauce, Green Beans with Celery Sauce, and Browned New Potatoes.

Oven temperature: 400°F. (hot).

Baking time: 25 to 30 minutes.

Yield: 6 servings.

PAPRIKA-BAKED FISH AND RICE

This requires very little effort to prepare.

1-1/2 tablespoons instant minced onion softened in 1-1/2 tablespoons water, or 1/2 cup chopped raw onion

2 cups cooked rice

4 tablespoons (1/2 stick) butter or margarine

1 pound fillet of haddock, halibut, perch, or other boned fish

salt

imported paprika

1. Combine onion and rice and mix lightly with a fork.
2. Spread rice mixture in a well-buttered 10 x 6 x 2-inch baking dish and dot with 2 tablespoons of the butter or margarine.
3. Wipe fish with a damp cloth and arrange fish over the rice.
4. Sprinkle 1/4 teaspoon salt and 1/4 teaspoon paprika over each serving of fish and dot with the remaining 2 tablespoons butter or margarine.
5. Bake in a preheated moderate oven until the fish flakes when tested with a fork.

6. Serve with Green Beans with Tomato Mayonnaise, Cabbage and Carrot Slaw, and French bread.

Oven temperature: 375°F. (moderate).

Baking time: 25 to 30 minutes.

Yield: 4 servings.

FISH BAKED IN SOUR CREAM

A delicious fish dish that is easy to make.

1-1/4 pounds fillet of haddock, halibut, pike or other white fish fillets	1/2 cup sour cream
	2 tablespoons butter or margarine, melted
3/4 teaspoon salt	3/4 cup soft breadcrumbs
1 teaspoon imported paprika	

1. Wipe fish with a damp cloth and cut it into 4 serving pieces.
2. Arrange fish in a buttered 10 x 6 x 2-inch baking dish.
3. Sprinkle salt and paprika over the fish and spread with sour cream.
4. Combine melted butter or margarine and bread crumbs and sprinkle over the sour cream.
5. Bake in a preheated slow oven until fish flakes when tested with a fork and crumbs are brown.
6. Serve promptly with Browned New Potatoes, Broccoli with Dilly Butter Sauce, tomato and carrot salad, and corn sticks.

Oven temperature: 325°F. (slow).

Baking time: 35 to 40 minutes.

Yield: 4 servings.

SAVORY BAKED FISH STEAKS

2 pounds fish steaks (cod, halibut, or swordfish)
salt to taste
_____
1/2 teaspoon powdered mustard soaked in 1 teaspoon water
1/2 cup mayonnaise
1 teaspoon lemon juice

1 teaspoon instant minced onion or 1 tablespoon finely chopped raw onion
1/2 teaspoon dried thyme leaves
1/8 teaspoon ground black pepper
_____
snipped parsley or paprika

1. Wipe fish with a damp cloth, cut it into 6 serving-size pieces, and arrange them in a buttered baking dish.
2. Sprinkle the fish with salt to taste.
3. Combine the next 6 ingredients and spread the mixture over the fish.
4. Bake in a preheated very hot oven until the top is well-flecked with brown.
5. Garnish with snipped parsley or paprika.
6. Serve with buttered whole-kernel corn, Broccoli with Browned Butter, tomato and cucumber salad, and hot Onion French Bread.

Oven temperature: 450°F. (very hot).

Baking time: 20 to 25 minutes.

Yield: 6 servings.

FILLET OF HADDOCK
BAKED WITH BREAD CRUMBS

One of my favorite fish dishes.

1-1/2 pounds fillet of haddock
salt
6 slices butter or margarine,
   cut 1/4 inch thick

3 cups soft bread crumbs
1 teaspoon salt

1/8 teaspoon ground black
   pepper
6 tablespoons (3/4 stick) butter or margarine, melted

parsley

1. Cut fish into 6 serving pieces.
2. Arrange the fish in a well-buttered 12 x 7-1/2 x 2-inch baking dish.
3. Sprinkle salt lightly over each serving and put a slice of butter on each.
4. Combine the next 4 ingredients and sprinkle the mixture over the fish, covering the pieces completely.
5. Bake in a moderate oven until crumbs have browned.
6. Garnish with parsley and serve promptly with buttered asparagus, Baked Carrots, Dilly Cucumbers, and hot Onion Hard Rolls.

Oven temperature: 350°F. (moderate).

Baking time: 30 minutes.

Yield: 6 servings.

POACHED FISH WITH MAYONNAISE

3 cups water
1/2 cup wine vinegar
2 teaspoons instant minced onion or 1 small onion, sliced
4 whole black peppers
1/2 small bay leaf

1-1/2 teaspoons salt
1/2 teaspoon sugar

4 servings (5 ounces each) fillet of haddock or halibut
mayonnaise
snipped parsley or parsley flakes

1. Put the first 7 ingredients in a 10-inch skillet and bring the mixture to boiling point.
2. Carefully place fish in the liquid, reduce heat, and simmer, uncovered, 8 to 10 minutes or until the fish flakes when tested with a fork.
3. Using a slotted spoon or pancake turner, transfer fish to a warmed platter.
4. Spread fish with mayonnaise, and sprinkle with snipped parsley or parsley flakes.
5. Serve hot with baked potato, buttered green beans, and Cabbage and Carrot Slaw.

Yield: 4 servings.

ROLLED STUFFED FISH FILLETS

1-1/2 pounds thin fillets halibut, haddock, or flounder
salt
Curry Stuffing (see following recipe)

1/4 cup hot water
2 teaspoons butter or margarine
paprika or snipped parsley

1. Wipe fish with a damp cloth, and cut it into 4 strips 8 x 3 inches.
2. Sprinkle fillets lightly with salt and spread each with Curry Stuffing to within 1/4 inch from edges at the sides and to within 1/2 inch from edges at the ends.
3. Roll up fillets in jelly-roll fashion and fasten the ends with small metal skewers or with toothpicks.
4. Place rolls in a buttered 10 x 6 x 2-inch baking dish.
5. Pour hot water into the dish around, not over, rolls.
6. Dot each roll with 1/2 teaspoon butter or margarine.
7. Bake, uncovered, in a preheated moderate oven until fish flakes when tested with a fork.
8. Spoon some of the pan juices over each serving, garnish with paprika or snipped parsley. Serve promptly.

Oven temperature: 350°F. (moderate).

Baking time: 30 minutes.

Yield: 4 servings.

CURRY STUFFING

2 cups soft bread crumbs (about 4 slices bread)

2 teaspoons instant minced onion

dash garlic powder

1/2 teaspoon salt

3/4 teaspoon curry powder

2 tablespoons butter or margarine, melted

1 tablespoon hot water

1. Combine the first 5 ingredients and mix well.
2. Add melted butter or margarine and hot water, and mix until well blended.

3. Spread the stuffing over the fish fillets.

4. Roll and bake according to preceding directions.

Yield: Sufficient stuffing for 4 fish fillets, 8 x 3 inches.

SALMON LOAF

1 can (1 pound) pink or red salmon
_____

1/2 cup fine dry breadcrumbs
1 tablespoon flour
1 teaspoon salt
1/4 teaspoon ground black pepper
1/4 teaspoon poultry seasoning

1 tablespoon lemon juice
2 large eggs, beaten
1 tablespoon bacon drippings, or butter or margarine, melted
_____

1/2 cup milk or tomato juice
Egg Sauce (see following recipe)

1. Turn salmon into a 2-quart bowl, flake it, and remove bones.

2. Add the next 8 ingredients and mix well.

3. Stir in milk or tomato juice.

4. Turn mixture into a greased 7-1/2 x 3-3/4 x 2-1/4-inch loaf pan. Smooth top with a spoon or rubber spatula.

5. Bake in a preheated moderate oven until the top is well flecked with brown.

6. Serve sliced with Egg Sauce or plain with new potatoes, green peas with Curry Butter, and Cabbage and Carrot Slaw.

Oven temperature: 350°F. (moderate).

Baking time: 50 minutes.

Yield: 4 to 5 servings.

EGG SAUCE

1 tablespoon butter or margarine

1 tablespoon flour

1 cup milk

1/2 teaspoon salt

1/16 teaspoon ground black pepper

1/16 teaspoon onion powder

2 large hard-cooked eggs, diced

2 teaspoons fresh lemon juice

1. Melt butter or margarine in saucepan. Stir in flour.
2. Add milk gradually along with the next 3 ingredients.
3. Stir and cook until slightly thickened. Add diced eggs and lemon juice.
4. Serve with Salmon Loaf, poached fish, or vegetables.

Yield: Approximately 1-1/2 cups.

BAKED SALMON MOUSSE

1 can (1 pound) pink salmon or red salmon, flaked and drained

2 large egg whites, unbeaten

1 tablespoon lemon juice

1-1/2 cups heavy cream, not whipped

1 teaspoon salt or salt to taste

1/4 teaspoon ground white pepper

fine, dry breadcrumbs

Mustard Sauce or Cucumber Sauce

1. Drain salmon well and put half in a 2-quart mixing bowl.
2. Add egg whites and lemon juice.
3. With an electric beater, beat the mixture until a fluffy purée is formed.

4. Add remaining salmon, cream, salt, and pepper and mix well.
5. Grease a 1-quart mold and sprinkle it with fine dry breadcrumbs, coating it completely.
6. Pour in salmon mixture.
7. Place the mold in a pan of hot water and bake in a preheated slow oven until puffed and soft-firm.
8. Remove the mousse from the oven and cool in the mold 5 minutes. Unmold the mousse onto a serving plate.
9. Serve with Mustard Sauce or Cucumber Sauce.

Oven temperature: 325°F. (slow).

Baking time: 1-1/2 hours.

Yield: 6 servings.

BAKED SMELTS

1 pound smelts

1/4 cup salad oil

1 teaspoon salt

1/8 teaspoon ground black pepper

1/2 teaspoon instant minced onion

1 teaspoon lemon juice

1/2 cup fine dry breadcrumbs

snipped parsley

1. Wash smelts, remove the heads, and arrange smelts in an 8 x 8 x 2-inch baking dish.
2. Combine the next 5 ingredients and pour the mixture over smelts.
3. Marinate 2 or more hours, turning smelts in the marinade 2 or 3 times.

4. When ready to bake the smelts, sprinkle with breadcrumbs and bake in a preheated hot oven until smelts flake when tested with a fork.

5. Sprinkle with snipped parsley and serve promptly.

Oven temperature: 400°F. (hot).

Baking time: 20 minutes.

Yield: 6 servings.

TUNA-FISH RAREBIT

4 tablespoons (1/2 stick) butter or margarine, softened

4 tablespoons flour

1 teaspoon salt

1 teaspoon chili powder (optional)

1/2 teaspoon powdered mustard soaked in 1 teaspoon water

2 cups milk

1 can (6-1/2 ounces) chunk-style tuna fish, flaked

1 cup shredded sharp American cheese

1/8 teaspoon ground black pepper

6 slices toasted bread

1. Put the first 5 ingredients in a 1-1/2-quart saucepan and mix well to form a roux. Add milk.

2. Stir and cook until the sauce is of medium thickness.

3. Stir in tuna fish, cheese, and black pepper. Heat only until the mixture is hot. (Do not boil.)

4. Serve over toast for lunch or supper with Grilled Tomatoes, and Endive and Spinach Salad.

Yield: 6 servings.

SHELLFISH

BOILED FRESH SHRIMP IN THE SHELL

1. Wash fresh uncooked shrimp and put them into a saucepan of boiling salted water to cover (1 teaspoon salt to 2 cups water).
2. Cook, covered, until shrimp turn pink, about 5 minutes. (Long cooking and high temperature toughen shrimp.)
3. Drain shrimp and rinse in cold water.
4. Remove shells and black vein which runs along the back.
5. Prepare as desired.

Yield: 1 pound fresh uncooked shrimp yields approximately 1-1/4 cups cooked shrimp.

Note: Shrimp that have been shelled and deveined may be cooked in the same way.

CURRIED SHRIMP

1 teaspoon instant minced onion softened in 1 teaspoon water or 1 tablespoon chopped raw onion

3 to 4 teaspoons curry powder

1/4 cup (1/2 stick) butter or margarine, melted

1/4 cup flour

2 cups milk

1/2 teaspoon salt or salt to taste

1/4 teaspoon ground black pepper

1/4 teaspoon ground ginger

3/4 pound peeled, deveined, cooked fresh shrimp or 2 cans (4-1/2 ounces each) shrimp

2 cups cooked rice

1. Add onion and curry powder to melted butter or margarine and cook, stirring, 1 minute over low heat.
2. Remove saucepan from heat, and blend in flour.
3. Cook, stirring, 2 to 3 minutes or until the mixture is foamy.
4. Remove from heat and add milk. Cook, stirring, until the sauce is medium thick, 4 to 5 minutes.
5. Add the next 4 ingredients. Cook, stirring frequently, over medium heat until shrimp are hot, about 5 minutes.
6. Serve over rice with 3 to 4 of the following accompaniments: chutney; sieved hard-cooked egg yolks; sieved hard-cooked egg whites; sliced toasted blanched almonds; diced apples; seedless green grapes; spiced fruit (apricots, figs, peaches, apples, watermelon rind); flaked coconut or shredded coconut; banana chunks, rolled in orange juice and then in flaked coconut.

Yield: 4 servings.

SAUTÉED SHRIMP, SOUTHERN STYLE

1/4 cup butter or margarine

1 teaspoon salt

1/16 teaspoon ground black pepper

1-1/2 pounds cooked fresh shrimp, shelled and deveined

3 cups cooked rice or cooked grits

1. Melt butter or margarine in a 1-1/2-quart saucepan.
2. Add the next 3 ingredients. Cook over low heat, stirring frequently, until shrimp are hot, 5 to 6 minutes.
3. Serve hot over rice or grits.

Yield: 6 servings.

CURRIED SAUTÉED SHRIMP

In the preceding recipe for Sautéed Shrimp, Southern Style, add 1/2 teaspoon curry powder to the melted butter. Proceed according to directions in the recipe.
Yield: 6 servings.

SHRIMP CHINESE STYLE

2 pounds raw shrimp, peeled and deveined

1/3 cup soy sauce
1/2 cup sauterne
3 tablespoons salad oil
1/2 teaspoon ground ginger

1/4 teaspoon instant minced garlic or 1 clove fresh garlic, split

1 tablespoon cornstarch
1/4 cup water
3 cups cooked rice

1. Rinse shrimp and dry them with paper towels.
2. Combine the next 5 ingredients in a 1-1/2-quart mixing bowl, add shrimp, and mix well.
3. Marinate, covered, in the refrigerator 3 to 4 hours or overnight.
4. To cook, turn shrimp and marinade into a 9- or 10-inch skillet. Cook, uncovered, over medium-low heat, 8 to 10 minutes or until shrimp turn pink, stirring frequently.
5. Blend cornstarch with water and add to the sauce. Stir and cook until slightly thickened, about 1 minute. (Remove raw garlic, if used.)
6. Serve over rice with crisp-tender braised zucchini squash and Tossed Orange and Onion Salad.
Yield: 6 servings.

QUICK SHRIMP NEWBURG

1 can (10 ounces) frozen cream of shrimp soup, thawed
1 can (4 1/2 ounces) deveined shrimp, drained
1 can (2 ounces) sliced mushrooms

3 tablespoons dry sherry
3 slices toast or 3 patty shells
snipped parsley

1. Put the first 3 ingredients in a 1-1/2-quart saucepan.
2. Cook over low heat, stirring frequently, until the mixture is hot.
3. Add the sherry and heat 1 minute.
4. Serve hot on toast or in patty shells, garnished with snipped parsley.

Yield: 3 servings.

CRAB MEAT NORFOLK

This dish may also be made with cooked shrimp or cooked lobster.

1/4 cup (1/2 stick) butter, melted
4 teaspoons lemon juice
1/4 teaspoon salt

ground black pepper to taste
2 cups cooked crab meat (fresh or canned)
paprika

1. Put the first 4 ingredients in a 1-quart casserole.
2. Add the crab meat and mix well.

3. Place in the broiler oven under moderate heat and broil 8 to 10 minutes.
4. Sprinkle with paprika. Serve hot.

Broiler temperature: 375°F. (moderate).

Broiling time: 8 to 10 minutes.

Yield: 4 servings.

COLD CRAB-MEAT MOUSSE

2 packages unflavored gelatin
1/2 cup cold water
1 cup boiling water
_____
1 cup heavy cream, whipped
1 cup mayonnaise
1/2 teaspoon salt or salt to taste

2 teaspoons lemon juice
2 cups flaked, cooked crab meat (fresh or canned)
2 tablespoons finely diced pimiento
_____
parsley and cherry tomatoes (optional)

1. Soften gelatin in cold water.
2. Add boiling water and stir until gelatin is dissolved.
3. Chill until the mixture begins to thicken, about as thick as fresh egg whites.
4. Fold in the next 6 ingredients.
5. Turn the mixture into a lightly oiled 2-quart mold.
6. Chill until the mousse is firm and ready to serve.
7. Turn the mold out onto a large serving plate and, if desired, garnish with parsley and cherry tomatoes.

Yield: Approximatly 10 servings.

MEAT

Meat is an important source of high quality protein, vitamin B, and minerals, whether it is an expensive cut or one of the less expensive cuts. All meat should be purchased with an eye for quality. The cuts should be well marbled with fat, the grain should be fine, and the color good. There should be a larger percentage of edible meat than of bone. Since seasonings on meat penetrate only slightly, thick cuts of meat, such as roasts, may be seasoned either before or after cooking, or both. Beefsteak, however, should never be salted before broiling since the salt will draw the juices.

HOW TO ROAST MEAT

Any tender cut of beef, lamb, pork, or veal may be roasted in the oven with dry heat. Season the meat with salt, ground black pepper, or other seasonings if desired. Place the meat on a rack in an open, shallow roasting pan, fat side up. The fat acts as a self-baster, and the rack holds the meat out of the pan drippings. If a veal roast lacks fat covering, cover the roast with thin strips of salt pork or strips of fat bacon.

Do not add water.

Do not cover.

Do not baste.

Roast in a slow oven (325°F.) according to the time given in the roasting timetables for various meats. An exception to this rule is beef tenderloin, which should be cooked in a very hot oven (450°F.) for a short time; see Timetable for Roasting Beef Tenderloin.

HOW TO USE A MEAT THERMOMETER FOR ROASTING MEAT

The meat thermometer indicates the internal temperature of the cooked roast. For perfection in roasting meat to taste — rare, medium, or well-done — follow these simple directions:

1. With a skewer, pierce a hole in the center of the meat.
2. Insert the meat thermometer carefully in the hole, but not against the bone, nor in gristle or fat.
3. Place the meat in the roasting pan and roast according to directions for How to Roast Meat.
4. As soon as the indicator reaches the temperature desired, the roast is done. Remove the roast from the oven.

HOW TO MAKE GRAVY

1. Transfer the cooked roast to a warmed platter and keep it warm while making the gravy.
2. Pour off the pan drippings and reserve 2 tablespoons of the drippings for each cup gravy you wish to make.

3. Return the reserved drippings to the unwashed roasting pan and add 1-1/2 tablespoons flour for each 2 tablespoons pan drippings. Mix well and scrape up all the browned bits from the bottom of the roasting pan.
4. Stir and cook to brown the flour lightly.
5. Add water. (1 cup for each cup gravy you wish to make.) Mix well.
6. Cook, stirring, until the gravy is smooth and is of the desired thickness.
7. Serve the gravy in a gravy boat.
8. Allow 2 cups gravy for 6 to 8 servings.

BEEF

Beef is the meat from mature cattle, usually steers. The lean should have a dull red color and a fine, velvety grain and should be well marbled with fat. The color of the fat should range from white to cream, while that of the cut ends of bones should be red.

ROAST BEEF

See directions under How To Roast Meat.
Allow 5 ounces bone-in beef roast per serving, 4 ounces boned beef roast per serving. A thin roast will require less roasting time per pound than will a thick one of the same weight.
For roasting times of various cuts, see Timetable for Roasting Beef on page 140.

TIMETABLE FOR ROASTING BEEF AT 325°F.
(Ready-to-cook weights at refrigerator temperature)

Cut	Weight (pounds)	Approximate roasting time (hours)	Meat thermometer reading (°F.)
Rib roast standing (bone-in)	4	1-3/4	140 (rare)
		2-1/4	160 (medium)
		3	170 (well-done)
	6	3-1/4	140 (rare)
		3-3/4	160 (medium)
		4-1/4	170 (well-done)
Rolled rib roast	4 (4-1/2 to 5 inches wide)	2-3/4	140 (rare)
		3-1/4	160 (medium)
		3-1/2	170 (well-done)
	6 (5-1/2 to 6-1/2 inches wide)	3-1/2	140 (rare)
		4-1/4	160 (medium)
		4-3/4	170 (well-done)
Rump roast (bone-in)	4	2-1/2	140 (rare)
		3	160 (medium)
		3-1/4	170 (well-done)
Rump roast (rolled)	4	2-1/2 to 3	140 (rare)
		3 to 3-1/2	160 (medium)
		3-1/4 to 3-1/2	170 (well-done)
Sirloin tip	4	2-1/4	140 (rare)
		2-3/4	160 (medium)
		3-1/4	170 (well-done)

BEEF TENDERLOIN

Beef tenderloin, the long muscle that lies along the backbone and inside the loin, is the tenderest of all beef cuts. It should be roasted in a very hot oven (450°F.) for a very short time. It is best served crispy-brown on the outside and rare inside.

TIMETABLE FOR ROASTING BEEF TENDERLOIN AT 450°F.
(Ready-to-cook weights at refrigerator temperature)

Cut	Weight (pounds)	Approximate cooking time (minutes)	Meat thermometer reading (°F.)
Whole tenderloin	4 to 6	45 to 60	140 (rare)
Half tenderloin	2 to 3	45 to 50	140 (rare)

POT ROAST AU JUS WITH VEGETABLES
(OVEN METHOD)

1-3/4 teaspoons salt
1/4 teaspoon ground ginger
1/4 teaspoon ground black pepper

3 to 4 pounds boneless pot roast (boneless chuck, rump, or sirloin tip)

1/4 cup hot water
1-1/2 cups canned tomatoes
1 cup diced potatoes
1 cup sliced carrots
1 cup diced onion or 1/4 cup onion flakes
1/2 cup sliced celery
1/2 cup diced green pepper

1. Combine the first 3 ingredients and rub mixture over all sides of the meat.
2. Place meat in a 4-quart casserole with a tight-fitting cover, or in a Dutch oven.
3. Put remaining 7 ingredients in the casserole or Dutch oven around meat.
4. Cook, covered, in a preheated slow oven until meat is tender.
5. Transfer meat to a warmed platter. Adjust seasonings in the gravy.
6. Serve meat sliced with some of the gravy spooned over it.

Oven temperature: 325°F. (slow).

Cooking time: 2 to 2-1/2 hours.

Yield: 6 to 8 servings.

SPIT-ROASTED BARBECUED BEEF

(OVER THE CHARCOAL GRILL)

1. Select a 3- to 4-pound, boneless beef roast (rolled boneless rib, rolled boneless sirloin, or eye of the round) not over 4 inches in diameter. Thickness of the roast, rather than weight, and heat of the burning embers determine cooking time.
2. Place roast on the spit and tie it firmly to prevent roast from slipping.
3. Mix 5 teaspoons salt with 1 cup hot water in a small saucepan and set aside on the grill to keep hot.

4. Cook roast slowly over a slow-burning charcoal fire; 2 to 2-1/2 hours for medium-rare, 3 to 3-1/2 hours for well-done.

5. Baste with the warm salty water at 10-minute intervals or as often as meat appears dry.

6. Begin basting meat with the following Hot Barbecue Sauce 30 minutes before meat has finished cooking.

Yield: 9 to 12 servings.

HOT BARBECUE SAUCE

2 teaspoons powdered mustard soaked in 1/4 cup water

1/2 cup cider vinegar

1/3 cup lemon juice

1/4 cup catsup

1 tablespoon brown sugar

2 tablespoons Worcestershire sauce

1-1/2 teaspoons salt

1/2 teaspoon cayenne

1/2 teaspoon ground black pepper

1 small clove garlic or 1/4 teaspoon instant minced garlic

1 teaspoon red-hot sauce or Tabasco

1 tablespoon finely chopped raw onion or 1 teaspoon onion powder

2 tablespoons salad oil, butter, or margarine

Combine all ingredients and bring to boiling point. Boil 1 minute.

Yield: Approximately 1-1/2 cups sauce.

BEEFSTEAK AND CHEESE ROLLS
IN TOMATO SAUCE

6 cubed steaks
salt and ground black pepper
  to taste
6 ounces sharp Cheddar cheese,
  cut into strips 3 x 1/2 x 1/2
  inches

2 tablespoons salad oil or
  shortening
Tomato Sauce (see following
  recipe)
cooked rice, noodles, or
  mashed potatoes

1. Sprinkle both sides of steaks lightly with salt and black pepper.
2. Place a strip of cheese across the center of each steak.
3. Roll up steaks, fasten the ends with toothpicks, and brown them on both sides in hot oil or shortening over brisk heat.
4. Add Tomato Sauce and simmer, covered, 30 to 35 minutes or until meat is tender.
5. Serve hot over rice, noodles, or mashed potatoes.

Yield: 6 servings.

TOMATO SAUCE

2 cans (8 ounces each) Spanish-
  type tomato sauce
1/3 cup water
1/4 cup chopped green pepper
1 tablespoon instant chopped
  onion or 1/4 cup chopped
  raw onion.

1 teaspoon dried oregano
  leaves
salt and ground black pepper
  to taste

1. Put the first 4 ingredients in a 1-quart saucepan and simmer, covered, 5 minutes.
2. Add oregano and salt and black pepper to taste.

Yield: Approximately 2 cups.

EASY COMPANY STEW
(OVEN METHOD)

2 pounds lean beef stew meat, cut into 1-inch cubes
2 cups cubed potatoes
1 cup sliced carrots, cut 1/2-inch thick
1 cup sliced onions
1/2 cup sliced celery
2 teaspoons salt

1 can (10-1/2 ounces) cream of mushroom soup
1 soup can (10-1/2-ounce can) dry white wine

1/2 teaspoon ground black pepper or black pepper to taste
snipped parsley

1. Put the first 8 ingredients in a Dutch oven or in a 3- or 4-quart casserole equipped with a tight-fitting cover. Mix well.
2. Cook, covered tightly, in a preheated slow oven 2 hours or until meat is tender.
3. Remove stew from oven and stir in black pepper.
4. Garnish with parsley and serve hot with Mixed Green Salad and Onion Corn Muffins.

Oven temperature: 325°F. (slow).

Cooking time: 2 hours.

Yield: 6 servings.

BEEF AND MACARONI CASSEROLE

3/4 pound (1-1/2 cups) ground lean chuck, browned lightly in 1 teaspoon butter or margarine

1/4 pound (1 generous cup) elbow macaroni, uncooked

1 cup (8-ounce can) tomato sauce

2 tablespoons instant minced onion or 1/2 cup finely chopped raw onion

1/2 teaspoon sugar

1/8 teaspoon instant minced garlic or 1/2 clove fresh garlic, crushed

1-1/2 teaspoons salt

1/4 teaspoon ground black pepper

2 beef bouillon cubes dissolved in 3 cups boiling water
_____

1/2 cup shredded sharp American cheese

1. Put the first 9 ingredients in a 2-quart casserole. Mix well.
2. Cook, covered, in a preheated moderate oven until macaroni is tender, 1 hour.
3. Sprinkle the top with shredded cheese and cook 10 minutes or until cheese has melted. Serve hot.

Oven temperature: 350°F. (moderate).

Baking time: 1 hour and 10 minutes.

Yield: 6 servings.

MY FAVORITE HAMBURGERS

1 pound ground chuck

onion salt

garlic salt

ground black pepper

4 pats butter or margarine

4 warmed hamburger buns

1. Shape unseasoned meat into 4 patties of equal size.
2. Sprinkle onion salt and garlic salt over both sides of hamburger and place them in a folding wire broiler or on the broiler rack of the oven broiler.
3. Broil over slow-burning coals or in the oven broiler until hamburgers have browned on both sides and to the doneness desired.
4. Sprinkle ground black pepper to taste over one side of each and top with a pat of butter.
5. Serve in warmed hamburger buns.

Yield: 4 servings.

CHILI CON CARNE

This dish has 271 calories per serving without rice, 372 calories with rice.

1 pound ground chuck (2 cups)

1/2 cup diced green pepper

2 cups canned tomatoes (16 to 17 ounces)

1/4 cup dehydrated onion flakes

1 teaspoon salt or salt to taste

2 cups undrained canned kidney beans (16 to 17 ounces)

2 to 3 teaspoons chili powder

1 teaspoon oregano leaves

1/4 teaspoon instant minced garlic

3 cups cooked rice (optional)

1. Cook meat with green pepper over moderate heat 5 to 7 minutes or until meat loses its pink color, stirring frequently.

2. Add the next 4 ingredients. Cook slowly, uncovered, 20 minutes, stirring occasionally.
3. Add all remaining ingredients except rice. Cook, uncovered, 5 minutes.
4. Serve hot, with rice if desired.

Yield: 6 servings.

HAWAIIAN MEAT BALLS

Easy-to-make flavorsome little meat balls perfect for the buffet table.

1 pound (2 cups) ground chuck, shaped into 1-inch balls

1/3 cup soy sauce
1/2 cup hot water

1 teaspoon ground ginger
1/8 teaspoon instant minced garlic or 1/2 small clove garlic, crushed

1. Place meat balls 1/4 inch apart in a 12 x 7 1/2 x 2-inch baking dish.
2. Combine remaining 4 ingredients and pour mixture over meat balls.
3. Bake in a preheated slow oven until meat balls have browned.
4. Transfer meat balls and some of the sauce to a chafing dish.
5. Place chafing dish on the buffet table and serve meat balls with toothpicks.

Oven temperature: 275°F. (slow).

Baking time: 1 hour.

Yield: Approximately 30 meat balls.

HAWAIIAN HAMBURGERS

1. Shape 1-1/2 pounds (3 cups) ground chuck into 6 hamburgers, and place them 1/2 inch apart in a 10 x 6 x 2-inch baking dish.
2. Combine the remaining ingredients in the preceding recipe and pour mixture over hamburgers.
3. Bake in a preheated slow oven until hamburgers have browned.

Oven temperature: 275°F. (slow).
Baking time: 1-1/4 hours.
Yield: 6 hamburgers.

OVEN CHOW MEIN

3/4 pound (1-1/2 cups) ground chuck

1 tablespoon salad oil, butter, or margarine

1 cup diced celery

1/2 cup raw rice

2-ounce can chopped mushrooms, not drained

3/4 cup condensed cream of mushroom soup

3 tablespoons soy sauce

1/4 teaspoon ground ginger

1 cup boiling water

1. Cook meat in oil, butter, or margarine over moderate heat until it loses its pink color, 5 to 6 minutes.
2. Mix meat with remaining 7 ingredients and turn mixture into a 2-quart casserole.
3. Bake, covered, in a preheated moderate oven 30 minutes.
4. Remove cover and continue cooking 30 minutes more.

5. Serve hot with buttered peas and Apple Cole Slaw.

Oven temperature: 350°F. (moderate).

Baking time: 1 hour.

Yield: 6 servings.

QUICK SPAGHETTI AND MEAT BALLS

1/2 cup finely diced celery

2 tablespoons instant minced onion or 1/2 cup chopped raw onion.

2-1/2 cups (1 pound, 4-ounce can) canned tomatoes

1 teaspoon salt

1/4 teaspoon ground black pepper

1/2 teaspoon ground Italian seasoning

1/16 teaspoon instant minced garlic or 1/2 small clove garlic, chopped

2 tablespoons tomato paste

1 beef bouillon cube
___

3/4 pound (1-1/2 cups) ground chuck

3 tablespoons fine dry bread crumbs

3 tablespoons water

2 tablespoons tomato paste

1 teaspoon instant minced onion or 1 tablespoon finely chopped raw onion

3/4 teaspoon salt

1/8 teaspoon ground black pepper
___

1/2 cup shredded American cheese

4 ounces spaghetti, cooked according to package directions

grated Parmesan cheese (optional)

1. Combine the first 9 ingredients in a 2-quart saucepan.

2. Cook, uncovered, 15 minutes.

3. Combine the next 7 ingredients in a 2-quart mixing bowl and shape mixture into 16 balls, 1-1/2 inches diameter.
4. Add meat balls to sauce and simmer, uncovered, 20 minutes.
5. Stir in American cheese. Heat only until cheese melts.
6. Serve over cooked, well-drained spaghetti. Sprinkle with Parmesan cheese, if desired.

Yield: 4 servings, 4 meat balls each.

BLENDER MEAT LOAF

If you own a blender, use it to make this delicious meat loaf. If a blender is not available, chop the vegetables very fine.

2 pounds ground chuck
1 cup fine dry breadcrumbs
1 tablespoon powdered mustard soaked in 1 tablespoon water
2-1/2 teaspoons salt
1/2 teaspoon ground black pepper

2 large eggs
1-1/2 cups diced tomatoes
2/3 cup diced green pepper
1 cup diced onion
1 tablespoon flour
1/3 cup cold water

1. Put the first 6 ingredients in a 2-1/2-quart mixing bowl.
2. Put 3/4 cup of the tomatoes and green pepper in the glass jar of the blender, blend 10 seconds, and add liquid mixture to meat mixture. Repeat, using remaining 3/4 cup tomatoes and onion, and add to meat mixture. Mix well.
3. Turn meat loaf mixture into a greased 9 x 5 x 3-inch loaf pan. With the fingers, pack the mixture down well.

4. Bake in a preheated moderate oven until meat loaf has browned and begins to pull away from the sides of the pan.

5. Cool meat loaf in pan 10 minutes. Drain pan drippings into a 3-cup saucepan.

6. Blend flour with water and add to pan drippings. Cook, stirring, until gravy has thickened. Serve in a sauceboat.

7. Turn meat loaf onto a warmed platter, slice, and serve with baked potato, Schnitzel Beans, and Sesame Seed, Apple, and Carrot Salad.

Oven temperature: 350°F. (moderate).

Baking time: 1-1/4 hours.

Yield: 8 servings.

GROUND BEEF MEXICANO

Easy and delicious. I suggest serving on Corn Meal Pancakes.

1 pound (2 cups) ground chuck

1/2 cup chopped green pepper

1/2 cup chopped raw onion or 2 tablespoons instant chopped onion softened in 2 tablespoons water

3/4 cup diced raw tomato, or 1/2 cup canned tomatoes

1 teaspoon salt

1/8 teaspoon ground black pepper

1/2 teaspoon crumbled dried oregano leaves (optional)

1 tablespoon flour

1/4 cup water or beef stock

4 slices toast or 4 Corn Meal Pancakes (see following recipe)

1. Cook meat in an 8-inch skillet over moderate heat until it loses its pink color.

2. Add the next 3 ingredients and cook, stirring, 5 minutes or until vegetables are soft.
3. Stir in salt, pepper, and oregano, if used.
4. Blend flour with water or beef stock until smooth and add to the meat mixture. Bring to boiling point, and cook 1 minute.
5. Serve over toast or Corn Meal Pancakes with Mixed Green Salad and sliced avocados.

Yield: 4 servings.

CORN MEAL PANCAKES

1 cup corn meal
1/4 cup sifted all-purpose flour
1-1/2 teaspoons double-acting baking powder
3/4 teaspoon salt

1/2 teaspoon sugar
1 large egg
1-1/4 cups milk
2 tablespoons shortening, melted

1. Put the first 5 ingredients in a mixing bowl and mix well.
2. Add egg and milk. Mix until all ingredients are blended.
3. Stir in melted shortening.
4. For each pancake, pour 1/4 cup batter onto a greased, hot griddle. Cook over medium heat until pancakes are brown on the bottom and bubbles form over the top.
5. Turn to brown on the other side. (Do not cook too fast.)
6. Serve with Ground Beef Mexicano and as bread for the meal.

Yield: Approximately 8 large pancakes.

LIVER LOAF

2 pounds beef liver or lamb or pork liver

3/4 cup boiling water

1/2 pound lean pork sausage

1 cup fine, dry breadcrumbs

1/2 cup finely chopped onion

1 tablespoon lemon juice

1 teaspoon salt

1 teaspoon Worcestershire sauce

3/4 cup liver stock

2 large eggs

2 strips lean bacon, uncooked

1. Put liver and boiling water in a 1-quart saucepan, cover, and simmer 5 minutes.
2. Remove liver from water and drain well. (Reserve liver stock to use later.)
3. Put liver through a food chopper, using medium blade.
4. Put chopped liver and the next 8 ingredients in a 2-quart bowl. Mix well, and turn mixture into a greased 9 x 5 x 3-inch loaf pan. Arrange bacon strips over the top.
5. Bake in a preheated moderate oven 50 to 60 minutes.
6. Serve hot with baked potato, Broccoli with Sesame-Seed Browned-Butter Sauce, sliced tomato, and whole-wheat bread.

Oven temperature: 350°F. (moderate).

Baking time: 50 to 60 minutes.

Yield: 10 servings.

LAMB

Lamb is the flesh of young sheep. It is always in season. The color is an indication of the age of the animal: young lamb has flesh and bones of a bright pinkish color and has fat which is creamy white or slightly pink. In older animals these colors become darker. Lamb should be cooked with care. Properly cooked, tender cuts of lamb are faintly pink, tender, juicy, and mild in flavor; the outside is well browned and the fat crisp. Overcooked lamb is leathery, grayish brown, and unappetizing. Tender cuts of lamb should be broiled or roasted. The less expensive cuts, such as neck, shank, and breast, should be braised or stewed. Lamb should always be served either hot or cold — never at intermediate temperature.

ROAST LAMB

See instructions under How to Roast Meat.
Allow 1/4 to 1/2 pound bone-in leg roast per serving; 1/2 to 3/4 pound bone-in shoulder roast per serving; 4 to 5 ounces boned roast per serving.
For roasting times of various cuts, see Timetable for Roasting Lamb on page 156.

TIMETABLE FOR ROASTING LAMB AT 325°F.

(Ready-to-cook weights at refrigerator temperature)

Cut of lamb	Weight (pounds)	Approximate roasting time (hours)	Meat thermometer reading (°F.)
Leg	6	3	175 (medium)
		3-1/2	180 (well-done)
	8	4	175 (medium)
		4-1/2	180 (well-done)
Crown (no filling in center)	5	3-3/4	180 (well-done)
Shoulder (bone-in)	3	2-3/4	180 (well-done)
	5	3-1/4	180 (well-done)
Shoulder (boned and rolled)	3	2-1/4	180 (well-done)
	5	3	180 (well-done)
Sirloin roast	2 to 3	2 to 3	180 (well-done)

ROSEMARY ROAST LAMB

1 carrot, peeled and sliced
1 rib celery, sliced
2 leeks or green onions (including tops), sliced
3 cups water

1 teaspoon crumbled dried rosemary leaves

about 2 teaspoons salt
1/2 teaspoon ground black pepper

6-pound ready-to-cook leg of lamb
3 tablespoons flour

1. Put vegetables and 1 cup of the water in the bottom of a large roasting pan.
2. Combine 3/4 teaspoons of the rosemary leaves, salt, and black pepper, and rub mixture over the surface of the roast.
3. Place roast in the roasting pan over vegetables.
4. Roast, uncovered, in a preheated slow oven until meat is tender, adding additional water if needed.
5. Remove roast to a warmed platter and keep warm. Remove excess fat from pan drippings.
6. Add 1-3/4 cups of the water and remaining 1/4 teaspoon rosemary leaves to pan drippings, bring mixture to boiling point, boil 1 minute, and strain.
7. Mix flour with remaining 1/4 cup water, add to pan drippings, and cook until gravy has thickened as desired. Adjust salt.
8. Serve with mashed potatoes or baked potatoes, Green Beans Amandine, and Avocado and Grapefruit Salad.

Oven temperature: 325°F. (slow).
Roasting time: Approximately 3 to 3-1/2 hours.
Yield: Approximately 12 servings.

SHISH KEBABS

(Cook over the barbecue grill or in the oven broiler.)

3 tablespoons salad oil
1-1/2 tablespoons cider vinegar
3/4 teaspoon salt
3/4 teaspoon garlic salt
1/2 teaspoon onion salt
3/4 teaspoon crumbled dried
   rosemary
1/4 teaspoon ground black
   pepper

2 teaspoons prepared mustard

1-1/2 pounds lean, boneless
   leg of lamb, cut into 1-inch
   cubes
12 of each of the following:
   onion slices, green pepper
   squares, small mushroom
   caps, and tomato wedges
frankfurter rolls or French
   bread, buttered

1. Put the first 8 ingredients in a 2-quart mixing bowl. Mix
   well.
2. Add lamb. Mix well. Cover and refrigerate 4 to 5 hours or
   overnight.
3. To cook, string 2 cubes of meat on each skewer, alternating
   with 1 onion slice, 1 green pepper square, and 1 mushroom
   cap.
4. Cook over slow-burning coals or in the broiler oven until the
   meat has browned and has cooked to desired doneness.
   Baste with the marinade as often as the meat looks dry.
5. To prevent overcooking the tomato wedges, string them on
   a separate skewer, baste with marinade, and put them on to
   cook when meat is half done.

6. Serve hot in buttered split frankfurter rolls, or in French bread cut to fit the kebabs.

Yield: 12 shish kebabs (6 servings).

DILLY LAMB CASSEROLE

2-1/2 pounds boneless leg of lamb or shoulder of lamb
2 tablespoons flour
about 2-1/2 teaspoons salt

1 bay leaf
1 teaspoon sugar

1 tablespoon cider vinegar
2 cups hot water

1 teaspoon dill seed
1/2 cup sour cream
1/4 teaspoon ground black pepper

1. Trim off excess fat from meat and discard.
2. Cut meat into 1-inch cubes and put in a 2-quart casserole. Add flour and salt and mix well.
3. Add the next 4 ingredients and 3/4 teaspoon of the dill seed.
4. Cook, covered, in a preheated slow oven until meat is tender.
5. Stir in remaining 1/4 teaspoon dill seed, sour cream, and pepper.
6. Continue cooking in the oven 5 minutes longer.
7. Serve with boiled potatoes, Cabbage Amandine, and cucumber salad.

Oven temperature: 325°F. (slow).

Cooking time: 2 hours and 5 minutes.

Yield: 6 servings.

ROSEMARY LAMBURGERS

3 slices white bread
1/2 cup water
1 pound ground shoulder of lamb

1 teaspoon salt

1/4 teaspoon ground black pepper
1/4 teaspoon crumbled dried rosemary leaves
1/16 teaspoon garlic powder

5 hamburger buns, heated

1. Soak bread in water 3 to 4 minutes. Drain off water, squeeze bread dry, and fluff it with a fork. Add to ground lamb.
2. Add the next 4 ingredients. Mix well, but lightly.
3. Rub the bottom of a heavy skillet with butter, margarine, or shortening, and heat.
4. Form lamb mixture into 5 patties, arrange them over the bottom of the skillet, and cook 15 minutes, or until cooked as desired, turning to brown both sides.
5. Serve between hot hamburger buns.

Yield: 5 servings.

OVEN-BRAISED LAMB SHANKS

1 cup sliced onion
4 lamb shanks (3-1/4 pounds)
4 medium-sized potatoes, peeled
8 medium-sized carrots, peeled

1 teaspoon salt

1 teaspoon dill seed
1/4 teaspoon ground black pepper
1/2 cup hot water
2 tablespoons flour
1/3 cup cold water

1. Put the first 4 ingredients in a Dutch oven or a 5-quart roasting pan equipped with a tight-fitting cover, in the order given.
2. Sprinkle salt, dill seed, and black pepper over all.
3. Add hot water. Cover tightly and cook in a preheated slow oven until meat and vegetables are tender.
4. Remove from the oven and transfer meat and vegetables to a warm platter.
5. Skim off and discard excess fat from the pan drippings.
6. Blend flour with cold water until mixture is smooth and add to the pan drippings. Stir and cook until thickened slightly, about 1 minute.
7. Serve gravy with the meat and potatoes.

Oven temperature: 325°F. (slow).

Cooking time: 1-1/2 to 2 hours.

Yield: 4 servings.

LAMB AND ONION CURRY

2 tablespoons butter or margarine
1 small white onion, chopped fine
2 teaspoons curry powder
1 teaspoon salt
2 pounds boneless, lean leg of lamb, cut into 1-inch cubes
18 small whole white onions, peeled
about 1 cup of hot water
1/2 cup sour cream
3 cups hot cooked rice

1. Melt butter or margarine in a heavy 3-quart saucepan.
2. Add chopped onion and curry powder. Stir and cook over medium-low heat 3 minutes or until onion is limp.

3. Add salt and lamb. Cook, uncovered, 5 to 7 minutes or until lamb loses its pink color, stirring frequently.
4. Add whole onions. Pour in hot water. Cook, covered, over low heat until lamb and onions are tender, about 1 hour, adding additional water if needed.
5. Stir in sour cream. Heat, but do not boil.
6. Serve for dinner over hot rice with fruit salad, and hot, buttered French bread.

Total cooking time: Approximately 1 hour and 10 minutes.
Yield: 6 servings.

CURRIED GROUND LAMB

Easy, economical, and perfectly delicious.

2 tablespoons butter or margarine or salad oil
2 teaspoons curry powder
1/2 cup chopped raw onion
1 pound ground uncooked lamb
3/4 teaspoon salt

1-1/4 cups hot water
1/4 teaspoon ground cumin (optional)
2 teaspoons ground coriander (optional)
2 cups hot cooked rice

1. Melt butter or margarine, or heat oil in a 9- or 10-inch skillet.
2. Add curry powder and onion. Mix well. Stir and cook until onions are very limp, 4 to 5 minutes.
3. Add lamb and salt.
4. Cook, stirring frequently, until lamb has lost its pink color, about 5 minutes.
5. Add hot water, and cumin and coriander, if used.

6. Cook, uncovered, over low heat 5 to 10 minutes.
7. Serve hot over cooked rice with 3 or 4 of the accompaniments listed under Curried Shrimp.

Yield: 4 servings.

CURRIED LAMB STEW

2 pounds boneless, lean shoulder of lamb, cut into 1-inch cubes

flour

4 medium-sized potatoes, peeled and quartered
12 small white onions, peeled
1-1/2 teaspoons salt or salt to taste

3 teaspoons curry powder
3 tablespoons tomato paste
1/8 teaspoon instant minced garlic or 1/2 clove garlic, crushed
1-1/2 cups hot water or hot lamb stock

2 teaspoons lemon juice

1. Cut off and discard excess fat from lamb and roll meat in flour.
2. Put meat and the next 7 ingredients in a 3-quart casserole, bean pot, or Dutch oven, equipped with a tight-fitting cover.
3. Cook, covered, in a preheated slow oven until meat is tender.
4. Remove stew from the oven and stir in lemon juice. Adjust salt, if needed.
5. Serve hot with Tossed Grape and Cabbage Salad or with Apple Cole Slaw, and hard rolls.

Oven temperature: 325°F. (slow).
Cooking time: 2 hours.
Yield: 6 servings.

PORK

While pork is available the year round, it is most plentiful and most economical in the late fall and the winter. It is available fresh, cured and smoked as ham or bacon, salted and as sausage. The color of young pork is grayish white, while that from older hogs is a delicate rose. The flesh is firm and fine-grained. Fresh pork should be thoroughly cooked to develop its rich flavor fully and to destroy a parasite, trichina, which is occasionally present.

TIMETABLE FOR ROASTING PORK AT 325°F.
(Ready-to-cook weights at refrigerator temperature)

Cut of fresh pork	Weight (pounds)	Approximate cooking time (hours)	Meat thermometer reading (°F.)
Loin	2 to 3	1-1/2 to 2	185
	5 to 7	3 to 4	185
Fresh ham (leg)	5	4-1/2	185
Shoulder (bone-in) picnic	5	3-1/3	185
Shoulder, bone-less rolled, picnic	4	3-2/3	185
Boston Butt (shoulder)	4	3-1/2	185

ROAST PORK

See instructions under How to Roast Meat.

Allow 5 to 8 ounces bone-in pork per serving; 4 to 5 ounces boneless pork per serving.

For roasting time of various cuts of fresh pork, see Timetable for Roasting Pork on page 164.

MARINATED PORK ROAST

4- to 5-pound pork loin or fresh ham

2 cans (10-1/2 ounces each) beef bouillon or 2-1/2 cups hot water and 4 beef bouillon cubes

1 tablespoon mixed pickling spice, tied in a bag

3 tablespoons cider vinegar or lemon juice

1-1/2 teaspoons salt

1-1/2 teaspoons poultry seasoning

2 slices lemon

1/2 cup sliced carrots

1/2 cup sliced onion or 2 tablespoons instant minced onion

flour

water

salt and pepper to taste

1. Put pork roast in a close-fitting pan or dish.
2. To make marinade, combine the next 6 ingredients in a 1-1/2-quart saucepan, bring mixture to boiling point, reduce heat, and simmer 3 minutes.
3. Pour hot marinade, including spice bag and lemon slices, over meat.

4. Add sliced carrots and sliced or instant minced onion.
5. Marinate meat in the refrigerator 24 hours, turning it 4 to 5 times to season meat uniformly.
6. Transfer meat to a deep roasting pan with a tight-fitting cover or to a Dutch oven.
7. Pour in marinade, including spice bag and vegetables. (Discard lemon slices.)
8. Cook, covered, in a preheated slow oven 2 hours. Remove cover and cook 1 to 1-1/2 hours or until meat is tender and brown.
9. Transfer meat to a warmed platter. Remove and discard spice bag.
10. Thicken gravy with flour blended with cold water until smooth, using 1-1/2 tablespoons flour and 1/4 cup water for each cup gravy desired. Add salt and pepper to taste.
11. Serve with mashed potatoes, Broccoli with Sesame-Seed Browned-Butter Sauce, applesauce, or Raw Cranberry Relish.

Oven temperature: 325°F. (slow).
Cooking time: 3 to 3-1/2 hours.
Yield: 6 to 8 servings.

PORK CHOPS WITH ORANGE SLICES

6 loin pork chops, cut 1-inch thick
1/2 teaspoon salt
1/4 teaspoon ground black pepper

6 unpeeled navel orange slices, cut 1/2-inch thick
butter or margarine
parsley

1. Wipe pork chops with a damp cloth and arrange them on the greased rack of the broiler pan.
2. Set oven control to *broil* and preheat broiler oven 5 minutes or until hot.
3. Place pork chops in the oven broiler 3 inches from source of heat. Cook chops 5 minutes on each side, or until seared.
4. Reduce heat to 325°F. (slow) and broil chops 15 minutes on each side.
5. Sprinkle chops with salt and black pepper.
6. Top each orange slice with 1/2 teaspoon butter or margarine and place 1 slice on each chop.
7. Continue to broil at the same temperature (325°F.) until orange slices are flecked with brown, 10 to 12 minutes. Garnish with parsley.
8. Serve with baked sweet potatoes or baked white potatoes, Green Beans with Celery Sauce, Tossed Grape and Cabbage Salad, and Poppy-Seed Rolls.

Yield: 6 servings.

PORK IN MEXICAN SAUCE

2 pounds lean raw pork
3 tablespoons flour
1 cup chopped onion
1/2 cup chopped green pepper
1 cup (8-ounce can) canned tomatoes
1/2 teaspoon sugar

2 teaspoons salt
2 tablespoons cider vinegar
1 tablespoon Worcestershire sauce
1 teaspoon red-hot sauce or Tabasco
3/4 cup water

1. Trim excess fat from pork and cut the lean meat into 3/4-inch cubes.
2. Put fat trimmings from pork in a 10- or 11-inch skillet, and cook slowly to try out the fat. Remove and discard cooked trimmings.
3. Dredge pork cubes in flour, add to hot fat in skillet, and cook until meat has browned, stirring frequently.
4. Add onion and stir and cook 5 minutes or until onion is soft.
5. Stir in green pepper and cook 5 minutes.
6. Add the next 7 ingredients, mix well, and cook, uncovered, 30 minutes or until pork is tender.
7. Serve with Cornbread, baked beans, or cooked rice, and green salad.

Yield: 6 generous servings.

PORK TENDERLOIN PATTIES

1-1/2 pounds pork tenderloin, cut into crosswise slices 2 inches thick

3/4 teaspoon salt

1/8 teaspoon ground black pepper

flour

2 tablespoons salad oil or shortening

1/3 cup hot water

1/2 cup sour cream

1. Flatten tenderloin slices slightly with a mallet.
2. Rub salt and black pepper over both sides of the patties.
3. Dredge patties in flour.
4. Heat oil or shortening in a 10-inch skillet, add tenderloin patties, and cook, turning to brown both sides.

5. Add hot water. Cook, covered, over low heat, 20 minutes or until patties are tender.
6. Stir in sour cream. Cook only until cream is hot.
7. Serve with baked potatoes, asparagus with Blender Hollandaise Sauce, and Mixed Green Salad.

Yield: 4 servings.

PORK WITH WATER CHESTNUTS

2 tablespoons salad oil
1-1/4 pounds lean pork, cut into 3/4-inch cubes
3 tablespoons soy sauce
1 cup hot water
1/2 teaspoon ground ginger
1/16 teaspoon instant minced garlic or 1/2 small clove garlic, crushed
1 can (5 ounces) water chestnuts, drained and sliced
1-1/2 teaspoons cornstarch
2 tablespoons dry sherry
2 cups cooked rice

1. Heat oil in a 10-inch skillet.
2. Add pork and brown it on all sides over brisk heat.
3. Stir in the next 4 ingredients.
4. Simmer, covered, until pork is tender, 35 to 40 minutes.
5. Add water chestnuts.
6. Blend cornstarch with sherry and add mixture to the pork. Stir and cook 5 minutes or until the sauce has thickened slightly.
7. Serve over cooked rice, with green beans with mushrooms and Tossed Grape and Cabbage Salad.

Yield: 4 servings.

HOW TO COOK HAM

There are several kinds of hams available in the markets today. They are:

Fresh ham, neither cured nor smoked. This must be thoroughly cooked before eating.

Country-style ham; usually smoked or heavily salted and peppered and cured several months. These hams should be parboiled before baking.

Cook-Before-Eating ham. These hams have been cured, smoked, and heated to an internal temperature of at least 137°F. Cook them thoroughly before eating.

Fully-cooked ham. These hams have been heated to an internal temperature of 148°F. They may be eaten without further cooking. However, if the ham is heated in the oven to 130°F., the flavor is improved.

Canned hams are fully cooked and boned. They may be eaten without further cooking or they may be glazed and baked about 10 minutes per pound.

Check the ham wrapper carefully for cooking directions. If there are no instructions, ask your butcher to tell you the kind of ham you are buying.

Allow 1/2 to 3/4 pound uncooked bone-in ham or picnic ham per serving; 5 ounces uncooked boneless ham per serving; 5 ounces cooked bone-in ham or picnic ham per serving; 2 to 4 ounces cooked ham per serving.

TIMETABLE FOR BAKING HAMS AT 325°F.

(Ready-to-cook weights at refrigerator temperature)

Type of ham	Weight (pounds)	Approximate baking time (hours)	Meat thermometer reading (°F.)
Fully Cooked	8 to 10	2-1/4 to 2-1/2	130
Bone-in, whole	10 to 12	2-1/2 to 3	130
Bone-in, half	5 to 8	1-1/2 to 2-1/4	130
Boneless, whole	10 to 12	2-1/2 to 2-3/4	130
Boneless, half	5 to 8	1-1/2 to 2-1/4	130
Cook-Before-Eating			
Bone-in, whole	8 to 10	3-1/4 to 3-1/2	160
	10 to 12	3-1/2 to 4	160
	12 to 15	4 to 4-1/2	160
Bone-in, half	6 to 8	2-1/2 to 3-1/2	160
Bone-in, smoked picnic	4 to 6	2-1/2 to 3	170
Smoked boneless Shoulder butt	2	2	170
Shoulder butt	3	3	170

GLAZED BAKED HAM

5- to 8-pound fully cooked half ham, bone-in

whole cloves

2 sticks cinnamon, each 2 inches long

1 cup pineapple juice or orange juice

1/2 cup honey, molasses, or light corn syrup

1. Wipe ham with a damp cloth. Trim off excess fat, leaving a layer about 1/2 inch thick.
2. Score fat. Insert a whole clove in the center of each square or diamond.
3. Place ham on a wire rack in a foil-lined, large, shallow baking pan. Insert a meat thermometer, if available, in the center of the ham, being sure that the point does not touch the bone.
4. Put cinnamon and fruit juice in a small saucepan, bring to boiling point, and boil 1 to 2 minutes.
5. Bake ham, uncovered, in a preheated slow oven 15 to 18 minutes per pound or until the meat thermometer registers 130°F. (1-1/2 to 2 hour), basting with the hot spiced fruit juice at 20 minute intervals.
6. About 40 minutes before cooking time is up baste with 1/4 cup of the honey, molasses, or corn syrup, and cook 20 minutes more.
7. Baste again with remaining 1/4 cup honey, molasses, or corn syrup and bake 20 minutes or until ham is golden.
8. Remove ham from the oven and cool. If desired, decorate with orange slices, pineapple slices, or maraschino cherries.

Oven temperature: 325°F. (slow).
Baking time: 1-1/2 to 2 hours.
Yield: 10 to 16 servings.

OTHER GLAZES FOR HAM

1. Prepare a 5- to 8-pound, fully cooked, bone-in ham for cooking according to preceding recipe for Glazed Baked Ham.
2. Bake the ham according to the directions in the recipe until 30 minutes before cooking time is up.
3. Then baste with one of the following glazes. Continue baking until ham is appetizingly brown, about 30 minutes.

MUSTARD GLAZE

1 tablespoon powdered mustard soaked in 2 tablespoons water

1/2 cup light brown sugar, firmly packed
1/3 cup light corn syrup

Combine all ingredients, and spread the mixture over ham 30 minutes before baking time is up.

MUSTARD-ORANGE GLAZE

1 can (6 ounces) orange juice concentrate, thawed
1/2 cup light brown sugar, firmly packed

1/2 teaspoon ground ginger
1/4 cup prepared mustard

Combine all ingredients and spread the mixture over ham 30 minutes before cooking time is up.

JELLY GLAZE

1 cup (8-ounce glass) apple jelly, red currant jelly, or guava jelly

1 tablespoon prepared mustard

2 tablespoons light corn syrup

1 tablespoon wine vinegar

Combine all ingredients and spread the mixture over ham 30 minutes before cooking time is up.

HAM LOAF

2 cups ground cooked ham

1 pound uncooked ground lean pork

1 cup crushed corn flakes

1/2 teaspoon salt

1/4 teaspoon ground black pepper

1 teaspoon powdered mustard soaked 5 minutes in 2 teaspoons water

2 large eggs, beaten

1/4 cup milk

parsley

orange slices or spiced peach halves

1. Put the first 8 ingredients in a 2-quart mixing bowl and mix well.
2. Turn the mixture into a greased 9 x 5 x 3-inch loaf pan, pat it down, and smooth the top.

3. Bake in a preheated moderate oven 1 hour.
4. Turn the loaf onto a platter and garnish with parsley and orange slices or spiced peach halves.
5. Serve with baked sweet potatoes, Green Beans Amandine, spiced fruit, Dutch Cole Slaw, and whole-wheat bread and butter.

Oven temperature: 350°F. (slow).
Baking time: 1 hour.
Yield: 8 to 10 servings.

VEAL

Veal is the meat from young cattle. It should have a grayish-pink color and a velvety, fairly firm texture. The bones are porous and should be red at the ends. Veal contains very little fat. It always should be cooked well done. The methods of cooking include roasting, braising, and stewing (never broiling). Since veal has a delicate flavor, it harmonizes with many more foods than do beef, lamb, or pork.

ROAST VEAL

See instructions under How to Roast Meat.
Allow 5 to 8 ounces bone-in veal per serving; 4 to 5 ounces boneless veal per serving.
For roasting time for various cuts of veal, see Timetable for Roasting Veal on page 176.

TIMETABLE FOR ROASTING VEAL AT 325°F.
(Ready-to-cook weights at refrigerator temperature)

Cut of veal	Weight (pounds)	Approximate cooking time (hours)	Meat thermometer reading (°F.)
Loin or rib roast	5 to 6	3-1/3 to 4	180 (well-done)
Leg (bone-in)	3	2	180 (well-done)
	6	3-1/3	180 (well-done)
Rump	4	2-2/3	180 (well-done)
Shoulder (bone-in)	5 to 6	3 to 3-1/2	180 (well-done)
Shoulder (boned and rolled)	3 to 5	3 to 3-1/2	180 (well-done)

VEAL PAPRIKA CASSEROLE

2 pounds veal stew meat, cut into 1-inch pieces
flour
2 tablespoons salad oil
2 teaspoons salt or salt to taste
2 medium-sized green peppers, sliced 1/4 inch thick

1 cup sliced raw onions
1 cup (8-ounce can) canned tomatoes
1 tablespoon imported paprika
2/3 cup hot water

1. Roll veal in flour and set aside.
2. Put salad oil in a Dutch oven or 3-quart casserole. Add floured stew meat. Mix well.
3. Cook, covered, in a preheated slow oven 1 hour.
4. Add remaining 6 ingredients and cook, covered, 1 hour longer.
5. Serve hot with riced potatoes or baked noodles.

Oven temperature: 325°F. (slow).
Baking time: 2 hours.
Yield: 6 servings.

TARRAGON VEAL

2 tablespoons butter or margarine

1/2 cup sliced raw onion or 2 tablespoons instant chopped onion softened in 2 tablespoons water

1-1/4 pounds veal stew meat, cut into 3/4-inch cubes

1 teaspoon salt

2 tablespoons flour

1/2 cup hot water

3/4 teaspoon dried tarragon or 1 tablespoon fresh tarragon

1/2 cup sour cream

2 cups cooked rice or noodles

1. Put butter or margarine and onion in a 2-quart casserole.
2. Cook, uncovered, in a preheated slow oven for 5 minutes.
3. Mix veal with salt and flour and add mixture to butter and onions. Mix well.
4. Cook, covered, in a preheated slow oven for 1 hour.
5. Remove cover, add hot water, and cook, uncovered, 20 minutes.

6. Stir in tarragon and sour cream. Cook, uncovered, 5 minutes, or only long enough to heat sour cream.

7. Serve hot over cooked rice or noodles with buttered broccoli and Avocado and Grapefruit Salad.

Oven temperature: 325°F. (slow).

Baking time: 1 hour 25 minutes.

Yield: 4 servings.

VEAL AND MARROW-BEAN STEW

1 cup dried marrowfat beans, washed well

3 cups water

_____

1-1/2 pounds boneless veal stew meat, cut into 1-inch cubes

3 medium-large carrots, sliced 3/4 inch thick

2 medium-sized onions, sliced 1/2 inch thick

1 medium-large green pepper, seeded and cut into lengthwise slices 1/2 inch wide

1 cup celery slices, cut 1/2 inch wide

1 cup (8-ounce can) thick tomato sauce

2-1/2 teaspoons salt

1/2 teaspoon ground black pepper

4 teaspoons imported paprika

1 small clove garlic, crushed, or 1/4 teaspoon instant minced garlic

_____

2 ounces salt pork (3 x 1-1/2 x 1-1/2 inches)

1. Put beans and water in a 3-quart saucepan. Cover, bring to boiling point, and boil 2 minutes.

2. Let beans stand, covered, in the hot cooking water for 1 hour.

3. Add the next 10 ingredients, mix well, and set aside.
4. Wash salt pork, score, and put it in the bottom of a 3-quart casserole or 3-quart saucepan.
5. Pour bean and meat mixture over salt pork.
6. If stew is cooked in the casserole, bake, covered, in a pre-heated slow oven until beans and meat are tender. If a saucepan is used, cook the stew, covered, over moderately low heat 2 hours or until meat and beans are tender.
7. Serve with Mixed Green Salad and Cornbread or crisp hot Garlic French Bread.

Oven temperature: 325°F. (slow).
Cooking time: 2 hours.
Yield: 6 generous servings.

VEAL GOULASH
(OVEN METHOD)

1 tablespoon butter or margarine or salad oil

1-3/4 pounds veal stew meat, cut into 1-inch cubes
1 tablespoon cornstarch
1 teaspoon salt
1 teaspoon dried oregano leaves
1/4 teaspoon ground black pepper
2 tablespoons snipped parsley or 2 teaspoons parsley flakes

1/4 cup instant chopped onion or 1 cup chopped raw onion
1 cup diced green pepper (about 1 medium-sized)
1 cup (8-ounce can) Spanish-type tomato sauce

1 beef bouillon cube dissolved in 1/4 cup hot water
1/2 cup sour cream
cooked noodles, rice, or mashed potatoes

1. Grease the bottom of a 2-quart casserole with butter, margarine, or salad oil.
2. Put the next 9 ingredients in the casserole and mix well.
3. Pour beef bouillon over all.
4. Cover and bake in a preheated slow oven 1 hour.
5. Remove cover and continue cooking until meat is tender, approximately 1/2 hour.
6. Remove casserole from oven and stir in sour cream.
7. Serve over cooked noodles, cooked rice, or mashed potatoes.

Oven temperature: 325°F. (slow).

Baking time: 1-1/2 hours.

Yield: 6 servings.

SHERRIED BRAISED VEAL

1-1/2 pounds veal stew meat, cut into 1-inch cubes
1-1/4 teaspoons salt
1/4 teaspoon ground ginger
flour
3 tablespoons shortening or salad oil

about 1 cup hot water
1/8 teaspoon ground black pepper
1/4 cup dry sherry
3 cups cooked rice

1. Mix veal with salt and ginger and dredge with flour.
2. Heat 2 tablespoons of the shortening or oil in a 10-inch skillet.
3. Add veal and cook over moderate heat until browned, adding remaining 1 tablespoon shortening or oil as needed. Turn veal occasionally to brown on all sides.

4. Pour in hot water. Cook, covered, over moderate heat, until meat is tender, abut 40 minutes. Add more water if needed.
5. Stir in black pepper and sherry. Simmer 5 minutes.
6. Serve hot over cooked rice with buttered spinach and Pear Waldorf Salad.

Yield: 6 servings.

VEAL-CARROT PATTIES

With these patties, children will get a portion of their daily vegetable requirement without knowing it. Ground chuck may replace veal, if desired.

1 pound ground veal
1 cup grated carrots
1/4 cup finely chopped celery
1 tablespoon finely chopped raw onion or 1-1/2 teaspoons instant minced onion

1-1/2 teaspoons salt or salt to taste
1/4 teaspoon ground black pepper
_____
1 tablespoon shortening or bacon drippings

1. Combine the first 6 ingredients in a 2-quart mixing bowl.
2. Shape the mixture into 6 patties.
3. Heat shortening or bacon drippings in a hot skillet, add patties, and cook until brown on both sides.
4. Cover the skillet and cook 5 minutes more or until patties lose their pink color.
5. Serve in hamburger buns, or as the meat course for lunch or dinner.

Yield: 6 patties.

RAGOUT OF VEAL WITH ALMONDS

Veal combined with tomatoes and currants, tastily seasoned with curry powder, and topped with toasted almonds is an elegant stew for a party.

1-1/2 pounds boneless leg of veal or shoulder of veal

3 tablespoons flour

5 tablespoons butter or margarine

3 teaspoons curry powder

2/3 cup chopped raw onion

2/3 cup chopped green pepper

1-1/2 cups water, veal stock, or beef stock

1-1/2 teaspoons salt or salt to taste

1-1/2 cups stewed tomatoes or fresh tomatoes, peeled and seeded

1/3 cup dried currants

1/4 teaspoon ground thyme

1/4 teaspoon ground black pepper

3 to 4 cups cooked rice

1/2 cup Toasted Slivered Blanched Almonds (see following recipe)

1. Cut meat into 3/4-inch cubes, dredge in flour, and brown in a deep 10-inch skillet or Dutch oven in 2 tablespoons of the butter or margarine.
2. Add 1 tablespoon of the butter or margarine and curry powder. Stir and cook 1 minute.
3. Add remaining 2 tablespoons butter or margarine, onion, and green pepper. Stir and cook slowly 5 minutes or until vegetables are soft.
4. Add water or stock and salt. Cook, covered, over moderate heat 30 to 40 minutes.

5. Stir in the next 4 ingredients. Cook, uncovered, until sauce has thickened and meat is tender, adding more water if needed.
6. Serve hot with rice, sprinkled with Toasted Slivered Blanched Almonds, chutney, diced apples, and spiced fruit.

Yield: 6 generous servings.

TOASTED SLIVERED BLANCHED ALMONDS

1. Melt 2 tablespoons butter or margarine in a 3-cup saucepan.
2. Add 1/2 cup slivered blanched almonds.
3. Stir and cook over moderately low heat until butter and almonds are straw color. Drain almonds on paper towels.

Yield: 1/2 cup.

PIES

In the United States, pie is probably the favorite dessert. In no other country do the cookbooks feature such a variety of recipes for pies. Since space limits the recipes included in this book, only a few of my most popular recipes will be found in this section.

FLAKY PLAIN PASTRY

(FOR A 1-CRUST 9-INCH PIE)

This method of making pastry is one you probably have never used. If the instructions are followed exactly, it makes a tender, flaky crust every time.

1 cup sifted all-purpose flour   1/3 cup shortening
1/2 teaspoon salt   3 tablespoons cold water

1. Sift flour with salt into a 1-1/2-quart mixing bowl.
2. With a pastry blender or 2 knives, cut in shortening until mixture forms flour-coated particles the size of peas.

3. Sprinkle water, 1 tablespoon at a time, over the flour mixture, tossing it lightly with a fork after each addition. Do not stir. This mixture will be crumbly.
4. Turn the crumbly mixture onto a flat surface and, with the hands, shape it into a mound.
5. With a spatula, cut the mound in half, and stack 1/2 of the mound on top of the other half. Shape this into a mound.
6. The mound will crumble, but keep mounding, cutting, and stacking the pastry until a satiny mound forms. The temperature of the day determines the number of times required to mound and stack the mixture.
7. With a lightly floured rolling pin, roll pastry on a lightly floured flat surface in an 11-inch circle about 1/8 inch thick.
8. Fold pastry circle in half and place it in an ungreased 9-inch pie plate.
9. Unfold and fit it carefully into the pie plate, pressing it against the inside walls of the pie plate to expel air bubbles. Do not stretch the dough.
10. The pastry should not extend more than 1/2 inch beyond the rim of the pie plate. Any additional pastry should be trimmed off with kitchen shears.
11. Turn under the edge of the pastry and press it against the side of the rim to prevent the pie crust from shrinking during baking.
12. Flute edge with the fingers or crimp it with a fork.
13. Fill and bake according to the directions given in individual recipes.

FOR PRE-BAKED PIE CRUST:

1. If pie crust is to be baked separately and filling cooked and put into the baked crust as with cream pies or chiffon pies fit pastry into the pie plate and prick bottom and sides.
2. Fit a smaller pan or a bean bag into the pie crust.
3. Bake in a preheated hot oven (425° F.) 12 to 15 minutes, removing the smaller pan or bean bag after pastry has baked 10 minutes. Bake until golden brown. Cool.
4. Add the filling as directed in individual recipes.

FOR UNBAKED PIE CRUST:

If filling is baked in the crust pour the uncooked filling into the unbaked pie crust and bake according to directions in the recipe.

FOR A 2-CRUST PIE:

For a 2-crust 9-inch pie double the ingredients, except use only about 5 tablespoons cold water. Bake according to directions in the recipe.

CHIFFON CREAM PIE

1 envelope unflavored gelatin
1/4 cup cold water
3/4 cup sugar
1/2 teaspoon ground mace
1 cup milk
2 large eggs, separated

1/4 teaspoon salt
1/2 cup heavy cream, whipped
9-inch baked pie crust
whipped cream, sweetened
Toasted Shredded Coconut
  (see following recipe)

1. Soften gelatin in cold water. Set aside.
2. Mix together in the top of a double boiler 1/2 cup of the sugar, the mace, milk, and egg yolks.
3. Stir and cook over hot water (not boiling) until custard coats a metal spoon.
4. Remove from heat, stir in gelatin, and place in a pan of ice water to cool.
5. Beat egg whites with salt until soft, stiff peaks form. Then beat in remaining 1/4 cup sugar, and fold egg-white mixture into custard.
6. Fold in whipped cream. Turn mixture into pie shell.
7. Chill several hours. Spread top with whipped cream topping and sprinkle with Toasted Shredded Coconut, if desired.

Yield: One 9-inch pie or 6 servings.

TOASTED SHREDDED COCONUT

Put 1/3 cup shredded coconut in a shallow pan and toast in a preheated moderate oven (350° F.) 10 to 12 minutes or until browned.

LEMON CREAM PIE

If desired, the filling may be served in sherbet glasses instead of being put into a pie crust.

1 cup sugar
2 tablespoons cornstarch
1/4 teaspoon salt

1 large egg
1/4 cup lemon juice
1 cup hot water

1-1/2 teaspoons vanilla extract

1/2 teaspoon grated lemon rind
1 cup heavy cream, whipped

9-inch baked pie crust, cold
unsweetened chocolate or shredded coconut

1. Combine the first 3 ingredients in the top part of a double boiler.
2. Beat in egg and then beat in lemon juice.
3. Gradually stir in hot water.
4. Cook, stirring frequently, over hot water (not boiling) until mixture has thickened, about 10 minutes. Cool.
5. Fold in the next 3 ingredients.
6. Turn mixture into the baked pie crust. Chill 10 to 12 hours or overnight.
7. Just before serving, shave unsweetened chocolate over pie or sprinkle with shredded coconut.

Yield: 6 servings.

LIME CREAM PIE

In the recipe for Lemon Cream Pie replace lemon juice and lemon rind with 1/4 cup lime juice and 1/2 teaspoon grated lime rind. Proceed according to directions in the recipe. Yield: 6 servings.

ENGLISH APPLE PIE

If this crustless pie is made the day before or several hours before it is to be served, it cuts into perfect wedges.

8 to 9 (3 pounds) tart cooking apples, peeled and sliced paper-thin
1/2 cup granulated white sugar
1/4 teaspoon salt

2 tablespoons lemon juice
3/4 cup brown sugar
1 cup sifted all-purpose flour
1/2 cup (1 stick) butter or margarine, softened

1. Combine the first 4 ingredients and pack them as firmly as possible in a 9-inch pie plate.
2. Mix brown sugar with flour in a 2-quart mixing bowl.
3. Add butter or margarine. With a pastry blender or 2 knives cut it in until mixture resembles coarse crumbs.
4. Sprinkle crumb mixture over apples and press down firmly, especially around the edges, to help the pie retain its juices while baking.
5. Bake in a preheated moderate oven until apples are soft and crumbs are brown.
6. Put a piece of foil on rack underneath pie to catch any juices that may boil over.
7. Serve cold cut in wedges.

Oven temperature: 350°F. (moderate).
Baking time: 1-1/4 hours.
Yield: 6 servings.

DEEP-DISH APPLE AND PRUNE PIE

5 medium-large cooking apples, peeled and sliced

1/4 cup boiling water

4 cups sliced, pitted fresh prunes

1-1/4 cups sugar

3 tablespoons quick-cooking tapioca

1/2 teaspoon salt

3 tablespoons butter or margarine

Plain Pastry, using 1 cup flour

1. Put apples and boiling water in a 2-quart saucepan.
2. Cover and cook until apples are about half done, 8 to 10 minutes.
3. Turn half-cooked apples into an 8 x 8 x 2-inch baking dish. Cover with the sliced prunes.
4. Combine the next 3 ingredients and sprinkle mixture over the fruit. Dot with butter or margarine.
5. Cover with a 10 x 10-inch square of pastry rolled 1/8 inch thick.
6. Trim pastry to within 1/2 inch beyond edge of dish.
7. Fold pastry edge under to form a standing rim around the edge of the dish. Using the fingers or a fork, crimp edge decoratively.
8. Cut 2 or 3 slits in the center of the pastry to allow for the escape of steam.
9. Bake until crust has browned and fruit is tender.
10. Serve warm or cold.

Oven temperature: 425°F. (hot).

Baking time: 40 to 50 minutes.

Yield: 8 servings.

PECAN PIE

This is not as sweet as most pecan pies.

3 large eggs, beaten lightly
1/2 cup light brown sugar
1/4 teaspoon salt
1-1/2 teaspoons vanilla extract
1 cup light corn syrup

2 tablespoons butter or margarine, melted
_____

1 tablespoon flour
1 cup coarsely chopped pecans
1 9-inch unbaked pie crust
whipped cream (optional)

1. Combine the first 6 ingredients in a large mixing bowl.
2. Blend flour with pecans. Add to egg and sugar mixture.
3. Turn filling into an unbaked 9-inch pie crust.
4. Bake in a preheated hot oven (400°F.) 15 minutes. Reduce heat to moderate (350°F.) and bake 40 minutes longer or until a knife inserted in the center of the pie comes out clean.
5. Serve cold. Top with whipped cream, if desired.

Total baking time: 55 minutes.
Yield: 6 servings.

OLD-FASHIONED PUMPKIN PIE

1 cup sugar
1/2 teaspoon salt
1 teaspoon ground ginger
1 teaspoon ground cinnamon
1/2 teaspoon ground nutmeg
_____
3 large eggs

1-1/2 cup mashed, cooked pumpkin (fresh or canned)
1 cup undiluted evaporated milk or light cream
1 unbaked 9-inch pie crust, chilled

1. Mix the first 5 ingredients together in a 2-1/2-quart mixing bowl.
2. Beat in eggs. Stir in pumpkin and milk.
3. Pour the mixture into the chilled, unbaked pie crust.
4. Bake 15 minutes in a preheated hot oven (425°F.). Reduce heat to 350° F. (moderate), and bake 35 minutes or until custard begins to set. Cool.

Total baking time: 50 minutes.
Yield: 6 servings.

OLD-FASHIONED YELLOW SQUASH PIE

In the recipe for Old-Fashioned Pumpkin Pie, replace pumpkin with 1-1/2 cups mashed cooked butternut or Hubbard squash. Proceed according to directions in the recipe.
Yield: 6 servings.

PUMPKIN CHIFFON PIE

My favorite pumpkin pie.

1 envelope unflavored gelatin
1/4 cup water
3/4 cup sugar

1/2 teaspoon ground nutmeg
1/2 teaspoon ground ginger
1/2 teaspoon ground cinnamon
1/4 teaspoon ground cardamom (optional)

1/2 teaspoon salt

1 cup mashed, cooked pumpkin

2 large eggs, separated
1/2 cup milk
9-inch cold, baked pie crust

1 tablespoon sugar
1/2 cup heavy cream

1. Soften gelatin in cold water and set aside.
2. Combine 1/2 cup of the sugar with the next 5 ingredients in the top part of a double boiler.
3. Blend in pumpkin, egg yolks, and milk.
4. Cook mixture over hot water (not boiling) until it is thick, stirring frequently.
5. Remove from heat and stir in softened gelatin.
6. Chill over ice water until mixture mounds when dropped from a spoon.
7. Beat egg whites until they stand in soft, stiff peaks, then gradually beat in the remaining 1/4 cup sugar.
8. Fold beaten whites into pumpkin mixture and turn it into the cold, baked pie crust.
9. Chill until pie is firm and ready to serve.
10. Add sugar to cream and whip until it stands in soft peaks. Spread over pie.

Yield: 6 servings.

RHUBARB PIE

Plain Pastry for a 2-crust 9-inch pie

5 cups diced rhubarb
1-1/4 cups sugar
1/4 teaspoon salt

3 tablespoons quick-cooking tapioca
1 teaspoon grated lemon rind
3 tablespoons butter or margarine

1. Line a 9-inch pie plate with half the pastry rolled to 1/8 inch thickness in an 11-inch circle.

2. Combine the next 5 ingredients and turn the mixture into the pastry-lined pie plate.
3. Dot with butter or margarine.
4. Roll remaining pastry to 1/8 inch thickness in an 11-inch circle and place it over the rhubarb filling.
5. Trim pastry to within 1/2 inch beyond the edge of the pie plate.
6. Fold edge of pastry under to form a standing rim around the edge of the plate. Using the fingers or a fork, crimp pastry edge decoratively.
7. Cut 2 or 3 slits in center of top crust to allow for the escape of steam.
8. Bake in a preheated very hot oven (450° F.) 15 minutes. Reduce heat to 350° F. (moderate), and bake 30 minutes or until crust has browned. Serve cold.

Total baking time: 45 minutes.
Yield: 6 servings.

STRAWBERRY ANGEL PARFAIT PIE

A beautiful, delicious pie.

2 teaspoons unflavored gelatin
cold water
3/4 cup sugar
2 teaspoons lemon juice
2 large egg whites
1/4 teaspoon salt

1 teaspoon vanilla extract
1 cup heavy cream
9-inch pie crust, baked and cooled
Strawberry Topping (see following recipe)

1. Soften gelatin in 3 tablespoons cold water in a custard cup.
2. Place cup in a small pan of hot water (not boiling) to melt. Let stand in the hot water until ready to use.
3. Mix sugar, lemon juice, and 3/4 cup water in a small saucepan (this is important).
4. Cook the mixture, stirring, until boiling point is reached. Cook without stirring, until a very soft ball forms when a little of the syrup is dropped in cold water. (If a thermometer is used, it will register 234° F.)
5. Meanwhile, beat egg whites with salt until they stand in soft, stiff peaks when beater is withdrawn.
6. Gradually beat the hot sugar syrup, melted gelatin, and vanilla extract into the beaten egg whites.
7. Whip 3/4 cup of the cream until it stands in soft, stiff peaks and fold it into the egg-white mixture.
8. Turn filling into a cold, baked pie crust. Refrigerate until filling is firm.
9. Spread pie with Strawberry Topping. Chill until topping is set.
10. Whip the remaining 1/4 cup cream, spoon 6 dollops on the topping, and put one of the reserved whole strawberries on each.

STRAWBERRY TOPPING

1 quart fresh ripe strawberries	2 teaspoons cornstarch
1/3 cup sugar	1/4 teaspoon vanilla extract

1. Wash berries and reserve 6 of the prettiest ones, with caps attached, to use as a garnish.
2. Slice remaining berries. (There should be about 3 cups.)
3. Add sugar and let berries stand 30 to 40 minutes.
4. Drain juice from sliced berries into a 1-cup measurer, adding enough water to make 1 cup. Spoon the drained berries over the pie.
5. Pour juice into a small saucepan, add cornstarch, and mix until smooth.
6. Bring mixture to boiling point and cook, stirring, 1 to 2 minutes or until mixture is clear and has thickened slightly.
7. Cool, stir in vanilla extract, and spoon the glaze over the berries. Refrigerate until topping has set.

Yield: 6 servings.

SWEET PASTRY TART SHELLS

1-1/2 cups sifted all-purpose flour

1/3 cup sifted confectioners' sugar

1/8 teaspoon salt

1 teaspoon grated lemon rind (optional)

1/2 cup butter or margarine

3 tablespoons milk

1. Sift the first 3 ingredients together into a bowl.
2. Add lemon rind, if used. Add butter or margarine and cut it in until mixture resembles coarse meal.
3. Add milk and mix lightly to form a dough.
4. Divide dough into 8 equal parts. Roll each on a lightly floured flat surface in circles to 1/16 inch thickness.

5. Fit pastry into 8 ungreased tart pans, measuring 2 inches across the bottom and 3-1/2 inches across the top.
6. Prick pastry at intervals with tines of a fork. Then put a piece of waxed paper, cut to fit the tart shells, in each. Put a few dried beans on the waxed paper. This prevents the tart shells from forming blisters during cooking. Remove waxed paper and beans 5 minutes before cooking time is up to permit tart shells to brown.
7. Bake in a preheated moderate oven 15 to 20 minutes or until tart shells have browned.
8. When shells are cold, remove from pans and fill as desired.

Oven temperature: 350°F. (moderate).

Baking time: 15 to 20 minutes.

Yield: 8 tart shells.

FRUIT TARTS

8 Sweet Pastry Tart Shells

1/4 cup cornstarch
1/2 cup sugar
1/16 teaspoon salt

2 cups milk
4 large egg yolks
1-1/2 teaspoons vanilla extract

about 1 cup raw raspberries, sliced strawberries, diced canned peaches or apricots, or seedless grapes, cut in half

Glaze for Fruit Tarts (see following recipes)

whipped cream (optional)

1. Make tart shells and set aside to cool.
2. Put the next 3 ingredients in the top of a double boiler or in a 1-1/2-quart saucepan. Mix well.

3. Heat 1-3/4 cups of the milk and add gradually to sugar and cornstarch mixture.

4. Cook, stirring, over boiling water or medium heat until mixture is very thick, 5 to 7 minutes.

5. Blend remaining 1/4 cup milk with egg yolks and add to the hot mixture. Cook over hot water (not boiling) or over low heat until mixture is about as thick as mayonnaise. Cool completely.

6. Stir in vanilla extract and spoon mixture into cooled, baked tart shells. Refrigerate 3 to 4 hours or overnight.

7. Before serving, arrange fruit over tops of tarts and glaze with one of the following glazes. Garnish with whipped cream, if desired.

Yield: 8 tarts.

GLAZES FOR FRUIT TARTS

JELLY GLAZE

Heat 1/2 cup apple jelly or red currant jelly with 1 tablespoon water until jelly melts. Spoon over the fruit. Will glaze 8 tarts.

FRUIT JUICE GLAZE

Blend 1 tablespoon cornstarch with 2/3 cup canned fruit juice or juice from cooked fruit. Stir and cook until juice is clear and has thickened slightly, 1 to 2 minutes. Add 1 teaspoon lemon juice. Will glaze 8 tarts.

POULTRY

The term "poultry" usually includes chicken, duck, goose, and turkey. Of these, chicken is the most versatile, hence this chapter includes only recipes for roasting the other three birds. The quantities and cooking times specified in these recipes are for fully dressed, ready-to-cook birds.

BAKED CHICKEN, MARYLAND STYLE

6 tablespoons butter or margarine
2-1/2-pound ready-to-cook chicken, cut into 11 pieces
2 teaspoons salt
1/4 teaspoon ground black pepper
1/2 cup flour
2 large eggs, beaten
1/3 cup soft breadcrumbs
Chicken Cream Gravy

1. Melt 2 tablespoons of the butter or margarine in a 13 x 9 x 2-inch baking pan in the oven.
2. Rub chicken with salt and black pepper.
3. Dredge chicken pieces, one at a time, in flour, dip in beaten egg, and then roll in breadcrumbs.

4. Arrange chicken pieces, as they are prepared, in the baking pan.
5. Break remaining 4 tablespoons butter or margarine into pieces and scatter them over chicken.
6. Bake, uncovered, in a preheated moderate oven until chicken is tender and has browned.
7. Transfer chicken to a warmed platter, and if desired make Chicken Cream Gravy from pan drippings.

Oven temperature: 350°F. (moderate).
Baking time: Approximately 1-1/4 hours.
Yield: 5 to 6 servings.

BLANKETED CHICKEN

2 broiler-size ready-to-cook chickens, 1-1/2 to 2 pounds each
1 teaspoon salt
1/4 teaspoon ground black pepper
2 tablespoons finely chopped green pepper

1 tablespoon finely cut chives or green onion tops
4 thin slices salt pork or bacon, each 3 to 4 inches long
Chicken Cream Gravy (optional)

1. Wash chickens and split them in lengthwise halves.
2. To help chickens lie flat in pan, break wing and leg joints, and pull wings and legs close to body.
3. Rub chickens with salt and pepper. Place chicken halves in buttered baking pan, not on rack, skin side up.
4. Sprinkle green pepper and chives or green onion over chick-

en, and place a thin slice of salt pork or bacon lengthwise over each half.

5. Bake in a preheated hot oven until chicken is tender and has browned.
6. If desired, serve with Chicken Cream Gravy, made with 3 tablespoons pan drippings.

Oven temperature: 400°F. (hot).
Baking time: Approximately 50 to 60 minutes.
Yield: 4 servings.

CURRIED CHICKEN AND RICE CASSEROLE

1 cup raw long-grain rice
3-pound ready-to-cook chicken, cut into serving-size pieces

3 teaspoons salt
3 teaspoons curry powder
1/4 teaspoon ground black pepper

2 tablespoons instant minced onion or 1/2 cup chopped raw onion
1 tablespoon lemon juice
2 cups boiling water

1. Soak rice 1 hour in water to cover.
2. Arrange chicken over the bottom of a 13 x 9 x 2-inch baking dish.
3. Drain rice and discard water. Combine rice with next 6 ingredients and pour mixture over chicken.
4. Cook, covered, in a preheated slow oven until chicken and rice are tender.

5. Serve hot with Tossed Avocado and Grapefruit Salad and Spiced Peaches.

Oven temperature: 325°F. (slow).

Baking time: Approximately 1-1/4 hours.

Yield: 6 servings.

GEDAEMPHTE CHICKEN

2/3 cup flour

3 teaspoons salt

1/4 teaspoon ground black pepper

1-1/2 teaspoons dried marjoram leaves

3-pound ready-to-cook chicken, cut into serving-size pieces

1/2 cup chicken fat

1/2 cup chopped onion

1 cup chicken broth or hot water

2 teaspoons paprika

2 to 3 carrots, peeled and sliced

3 tablespoons chopped parsley

Poppy Seed Noodles (see following recipe)

1. Put the first 4 ingredients into a clean paper bag and shake the bag well.
2. Drop 3 to 4 pieces of chicken at a time into the bag and shake it, to coat the chicken well.
3. Melt 4 tablespoons of the chicken fat in a 9- or 10-inch heavy-bottom skillet.
4. Add chicken pieces to the hot fat and brown them on both sides, adding additional chicken fat as needed.
5. Place pieces, as they brown, in a Dutch oven or heavy-bottom saucepan. Add the next 5 ingredients and pan

drippings from skillet, scraping up all the browned particles. Cover and simmer 1 hour.
6. Serve hot with Poppy Seed Noodles.
Yield: 6 servings.

POPPY SEED NOODLES

An easy method of cooking noodles when a slow or moderate
oven is in use for another dish.

2 cups raw noodles

1 tablespoon salad oil
3/4 teaspoon salt
1-3/4 cups hot water

2 teaspoons poppy seed
2 tablespoons butter or margarine (or chicken fat)

1. Put noodles in a colander and rinse off excess starch under
   hot running water.
2. Turn noodles into a 1-1/2-quart casserole and add the next 3
   ingredients.
3. Cook, covered, in a preheated slow or moderate oven until
   noodles are soft.
4. Turn cooked noodles into a colander and drain off excess
   water. Return to casserole or turn into a serving dish. Set
   aside.
5. In the meantime, put poppy seed in a small saucepan. Stir
   and cook over low heat about 1 minute. Add them to
   noodles with butter, margarine, or chicken fat. Toss lightly.
Oven temperature: 325°F. (slow), or 350°F. (moderate).
Baking time: 20 minutes in moderate oven, 25 in slow oven.
Yield: 4 to 5 servings.

TARRAGON CHICKEN
(OVEN METHOD)

3 tablespoons butter or margarine

6 chicken legs (drumsticks and thighs)

2 teaspoons salt

1/4 teaspoon ground black pepper

1/2 cup chopped raw onion or 2 tablespoons instant chopped onion soaked in 2 tablespoons water

1-1/4 teaspoons dried tarragon leaves

3 tablespoons flour

1 cup chicken broth

1 cup sour cream

cooked rice or noodles

snipped parsley

1. Butter a 14 x 10 x 2-inch baking pan with 1 tablespoon of the butter or margarine.
2. Rub chicken legs with salt and black pepper and place them in buttered baking pan.
3. Sprinkle onion and 1 teaspoon of the tarragon over chicken and dot with remaining 2 tablespoons butter or margarine.
4. Bake, covered, in a preheated slow oven 1 hour or until tender. Remove cover and bake 15 minutes longer.
5. Transfer chicken to another pan. Keep warm.
6. Blend flour with chicken broth and add mixture to pan drippings. Mix well; stir in remaining 1/4 teaspoon tarragon leaves. Cook, stirring, 3 to 4 minutes.
7. Stir in sour cream. Return chicken to the baking pan, and heat. (Do not boil.)

8. Serve over cooked rice or noodles. Garnish with snipped parsley.

Oven temperature: 325°F. (slow).

Baking time: 1-1/4 hours.

Yield: 6 servings.

PAPRIKA CHICKEN
(OVEN METHOD)

2 tablespoons butter or margarine

3-pound ready-to-cook chicken, quartered

salt

flour

1/4 cup instant chopped onion, softened in 1/4 cup water, or 3/4 cup chopped raw onion

imported paprika

3/4 cup sour cream

3 tablespoons hot water

cooked noodles or rice

1. Butter the bottom of a 9 x 9 x 2-inch baking pan with 1 tablespoon of the butter or margarine. Set aside.
2. Wash chicken and drain well.
3. Rub chicken with 1-1/2 teaspoons salt and dredge it lightly with flour.
4. Place chicken in baking pan and sprinkle with onions.
5. Put 1 tablespoon paprika in a small sieve. Sift it over chicken. Dot chicken with remaining 1 tablespoon butter or margarine.
6. Bake, covered, in a slow oven for 1 hour. Remove cover and bake 15 minutes longer.
7. Transfer chicken to a warmed platter. Keep warm.

8. Add sour cream and hot water to pan drippings. Mix well. Heat, stirring, until sauce is hot. (Do not boil.) Add salt and paprika to taste. Serve from a gravy boat.
9. Serve promptly over cooked noodles or rice.

Oven temperature: 325°F. (slow).

Baking time: 1 hour 15 minutes.

Yield: 4 servings.

POLYNESIAN CHICKEN

An exotic dish appropriate to serve to guests as well as to the family.   The chicken may be browned ahead of time and finished cooking 30 minutes before serving.

2 tablespoons salad oil
3-pound ready-to-cook chicken, cut in serving-size pieces
1 can (5 ounces) water chestnuts, drained and sliced

3 tablespoons soy sauce
1/4 cup hot water
4 tablespoons sherry
2-1/2 teaspoons cornstarch
3 cups hot cooked rice

1. Spread oil over the bottom of a 13 x 9 x 2-inch baking pan.
2. Place chicken in pan, leaving a little space between pieces.
3. Cook chicken, uncovered, in a preheated hot oven 30 minutes. Turn chicken and cook 30 minutes longer.
4. Sprinkle sliced chestnuts, soy sauce, hot water, and 3 tablespoons of the sherry over chicken.
5. Return chicken to oven. Cook, covered, 30 minutes.
6. Transfer chicken to a warmed platter. Keep it warm.
7. Blend cornstarch with remaining 1 tablespoon sherry, add mixture to pan liquid, and mix well.

8. Cook, stirring, over surface heat, until the sauce has thickened slightly.
9. Serve the sauce in a sauceboat and spoon it over chicken and rice.

Oven temperature: 400°F. (hot).
Baking time: 1-1/2 hours.
Yield: 6 servings.

SOUTHERN FRIED CHICKEN

2-1/2-pound   ready-to-cook   1/2 teaspoon ground black
  chicken   pepper
3/4 cup flour, unsifted   1/3 to 1/2 cup shortening
2 teaspoons salt   Chicken Cream Gravy

1. Wash the chicken and cut it into 11 pieces (2 wings, 2 thighs, 2 drumsticks, 2 sides, 1 breast, 1 wishbone, and 1 back).
2. Combine the next 3 ingredients and dredge each piece of chicken in the mixture.
3. Heat 1/3 cup shortening in an 11 or 12-inch heavy skillet, or 1/4 cup shortening in each of 2 heavy 8 or 9-inch skillets.
4. Arrange dredged chicken pieces in a single layer over the bottom of the skillet or skillets.
5. Cook uncovered, over medium heat 45 to 50 minutes or until chicken is golden brown and tender, turning to brown both sides. Add more shortening if needed.
6. Remove chicken to a warmed platter. Make Chicken Cream Gravy from the pan drippings.

7. Serve hot with mashed white potatoes or rice, Green Beans Amandine, and Jellied Raw-Cranberry Salad.

Yield: 5 servings.

DEVILED CHICKEN LEGS

6 chicken legs (drumsticks and thighs)

2 tablespoons instant chopped onion or 1/2 cup finely diced raw onion

1/2 cup diced green pepper

1/4 cup chopped green olives or pimiento-stuffed olives

2 tablespoons cornstarch

1 tablespoon cider vinegar

1 teaspoon red hot sauce or Tabasco sauce

1/2 teaspoon instant minced garlic or 1/2 clove garlic, mashed

1-1/4 cups hot chicken broth (homemade or canned)

1 teaspoon salt

3 cups cooked rice

1. Arrange chicken legs in a 13 x 9 x 2-inch baking dish.
2. Combine the next 9 ingredients and pour the mixture over the chicken legs.
3. Cover dish with foil or with a cooky sheet. Bake in a preheated moderate oven until chicken is tender.
4. Serve hot with rice.

Oven temperature: 350°F. (moderate).

Baking time: 1 hour.

Yield: 6 servings.

HOW TO STUFF AND TRUSS POULTRY

1. Rub inside of the bird with salt, using 1/8 teaspoon salt per pound of bird.

2. If bird is to be stuffed, allow approximately 1 cup stuffing for each pound of bird.
3. Spoon stuffing loosely into neck and body cavities to allow room for expansion during cooking. Stuff the neck first.
4. Fold neck skin onto the back; fasten with skewers.
5. Spoon remaining stuffing loosely into body cavity.
6. Close body cavity by inserting 3 or 4 metal skewers through skin at the edge of one side of opening, having them pass over through the skin on opposite side.
7. Draw edges of opening together with a clean white string. Begin at the end of opening farthest from tail and lace the string around ends of skewers to draw edges of opening together.
8. Fasten the string around the tail to complete closing.
9. Press legs closely against the body of the bird, tie ends of leg bones together, and fasten string to the tail.
10. If bird is not stuffed and there is a band of skin across opening of body cavity, push ends of legs under it. This holds the legs in place.
11. Twist tips of the wings and fold tips under and press them against the back — akimbo style, so that wings lie flat.
12. Remove all skewers and string before serving.

HOW TO ROAST CHICKEN OR TURKEY

1. If a meat thermometer is used, insert it into the thigh next to the body. (This area requires the longest cooking time.) Make sure that the thermometer does not touch the bone.
2. Place bird, breast side up, on a rack in an open pan.
3. Rub skin with salt and softened butter or margarine.

4. Melt butter, margarine, or shortening in hot water, using 1 stick butter or margarine or 1/2 cup shortening to 1-1/2 cups hot water.

5. Cut 2 or 3 thicknesses of cheesecloth large enough to cover

TIMETABLE FOR ROASTING STUFFED CHICKEN AND TURKEY AT 325°F.

(Ready-to-cook weights at refrigerator temperature)

Kind	Weight (pounds)	Roasting time (hours)	Meat thermometer reading (°F.)
Chicken			
Broiling or frying	1-1/2 to 2-1/2	1-1/4 to 2*	190
Roasting	2-1/2 to 4-1/2	2 to 3-1/2*	190
Capon	4 to 8	3 to 5	190
Turkey			
Very young	4 to 8	3 to 4-1/2	190
Roasting (young	6 to 12	3-1/2 to 5	190
adult, hen or tom)	12 to 16	5 to 6	190
	16 to 20	6 to 7-1/2	190
	20 to 24	7-1/2 to 9	190

*If whole chicken is roasted without stuffing, oven may be set to 400°F. (hot) and roasting time cut by 1/2 hour.

bird loosely. Wring the cloths out lightly in the water in which the fat was melted (it should not be hot enough to burn the hands).

6. Spread the cloth loosely over the bird, covering it completely.

7. If breast and legs or wings tend to brown before the rest of the bird, cover these parts with foil.

8. Roast according to the timetable on page 210.

HOW TO ROAST DUCK OR GOOSE

1. Place trussed duck or goose (stuffed or not stuffed) breast side up on a rack in a shallow open pan. (Use a jelly-roll pan, if available.)

2. Place in a preheated slow oven and roast according to the following timetable.

3. Siphon off the fat as it accumulates in the pan. It is not necessary to prick the skin of the bird when cooked at this low temperature.

TIMETABLE FOR ROASTING DUCK AND GOOSE AT 325°F.

(Ready-to-cook weights at refrigerator temperature)

Kind	Weight (pounds)	Roasting time (hours)
Duck (not stuffed)	4 to 5	1-1/2 to 2
(stuffed)	4 to 5	2-1/2 to 3
Goose (stuffed)	8 to 10	4 to 4-1/2

STUFFINGS

ALMOND STUFFING
(FOR TURKEY)

1 cup blanched almonds, sliced and toasted

2 quarts (8 cups) toasted small bread cubes (croutons)

1/2 cup diced celery

3 tablespoons instant chopped onion or 3/4 cup chopped raw onion

1/4 cup snipped parsley

2 teaspoons salt or salt to taste

1-1/2 teaspoons ground thyme or thyme to taste

_____

1/2 cup (1 stick) butter or margarine, melted

1/2 to 3/4 cup turkey broth or chicken broth, or 1 chicken bouillon cube dissolved in 1/2 cup or 3/4 cup hot water

1. Combine the first 7 ingredients, add butter or margarine, and mix well.
2. Add only enough broth to moisten the mixture.
3. Spoon mixture into the crop and body cavities of a 10- to 12-pound ready-to-cook turkey.
4. Close body cavities with skewers and lace tightly with string.
5. Roast according to directions for roasting turkey.

Yield: Sufficient stuffing for a 10- to 12-pound ready-to-cook turkey.

CHESTNUT STUFFING:

Replace almonds in recipe for Almond Stuffing with 1 cup toasted, chopped, peeled chestnuts.

TO TOAST CHESTNUTS

Put chopped chestnuts in a shallow pan and toast in a preheated moderate oven (350°F.) 20 to 25 minutes.

CORNBREAD STUFFING
(FOR TURKEY)

5 cups toasted cornbread crumbs

3 cups toasted bread cubes (croutons)

1/2 cup chopped celery

2 tablespoons instant chopped onion or 1/2 cup chopped raw onion

1/4 cup snipped parsley

2 teaspoons salt or salt to taste

2 teaspoons poultry seasoning

1/2 teaspoon ground black pepper

1/2 cup (1 stick) butter or margarine, melted

1/2 cup chicken broth or turkey broth

1. Combine all ingredients. Spoon mixture into crop and body cavities of a 10- to 12-pound ready-to-cook turkey. Close cavity openings with skewers and lace tightly with string.
2. Roast according to directions for roasting turkey.

Yield: Sufficient stuffing for a 10- to 12-pound turkey.

CORNBREAD STUFFING FOR CHICKEN

Make half the Cornbread Stuffing recipe. Spoon mixture into the crop and body cavities of a 5- to 6-pound ready-to-cook chicken or capon.

Yield: Sufficient stuffing for a 5- to 6-pound ready-to-cook chicken or capon.

ONION STUFFING
(FOR TURKEY)

2-1/2 quarts (10 cups) toasted dry bread cubes (croutons)

1/4 cup instant chopped onion or 1 cup chopped raw onion

1/2 cup chopped celery

1/4 cup snipped parsley

2 teaspoons salt

2 teaspoons ground sage or sage to taste

1/2 teaspoon ground black pepper

1-1/4 cups (2-1/2 sticks) butter or margarine, melted

1/2 cup turkey stock or 1 chicken bouillon cube dissolved in 1/2 cup hot water

1. Combine all ingredients in a 4-quart mixing bowl.
2. Spoon mixture into the crop and body cavities of a 12- to 15-pound turkey.
3. Close cavity openings with skewers and lace tightly with string.
4. Roast according to directions for roasting turkey.

Yield: Sufficient stuffing for a 12 to 15-pound turkey.

POTATO STUFFING
(FOR DUCK OR CHICKEN)

3 cups hot mashed potatoes

1 cup dry breadcrumbs

3 tablespoons bacon drippings

2 tablespoons instant minced onion or 1/2 cup chopped raw onion

1-1/2 teaspoons salt

3/4 teaspoon poultry seasoning

1/8 teaspoon ground black pepper

1/3 cup diced celery

1 large egg, beaten lightly

1. Combine all ingredients. Spoon mixture into crop and body cavities of a 4 to 5-pound roasting chicken or duck.
2. Close openings and roast according to directions for roasting chicken or duck.

Yield: Stuffing for a 4 to 5-pound ready-to-cook chicken or duck.

POTATO STUFFING FOR GOOSE

Double the preceding recipe for Potato Stuffing. Spoon mixture into the crop and body cavities of a 10-pound ready-to-cook goose. Close openings, and roast according to directions for roasting goose.

GRAVIES

GIBLET GRAVY

While this is not the conventional method for making gravy, the result is excellent, and because the gravy can be made ahead of time, this method decreases the last-minute duties of preparing and serving a roast turkey or chicken dinner.

1. Wash turkey or chicken giblets (neck, gizzard, heart, and liver).
2. Place neck, gizzard, and heart in a 2-quart saucepan. (Reserve the liver.) If a richer stock is desired, buy a few chicken necks and add them.
3. Add cold water to cover. Add 1 teaspoon salt, 3 black peppercorns, and 1 slice medium-sized onion to each quart water used.

4. Bring water to boiling point, reduce heat, and simmer, covered, about 1-1/2 hours.

5. Add the reserved liver; simmer 15 to 20 minutes longer.

6. Remove saucepan from heat, and transfer giblets to a bowl. Cool stock and giblets.

7. Thicken stock with flour, using 1-1/2 tablespoons flour for each cup of stock. First add flour to 1/4 to 1/3 of the cold stock you plan to use. Beat until mixture is free of lumps. Blend with remaining stock. Stir and cook until gravy is of desired thickness.

8. Chop the heart, gizzard, and liver and add to gravy (1/4 to 1/3 cup chopped giblets to each cup gravy). Reserve the neck for other uses. Refrigerate gravy or put it in a cold place until just before serving.

9. When turkey or chicken is done, transfer to a warmed platter. Keep warm.

10. Skim off and discard fat from pan drippings. Add drippings and browned particles scraped from bottom of roasting pan to previously made gravy to add flavor and rich brown color. Adjust salt and black pepper. Heat and serve in a gravy boat.

Allow 2 cups gravy for 6 servings.

CHICKEN CREAM GRAVY

3 tablespoons flour
pan drippings from baked or
  fried chicken
1 cup milk or light cream and
1 cup chicken broth, or 2
  cups milk
salt and ground black pepper
  to taste

1. Blend flour with pan drippings, scraping up all the browned particles from the bottom of the pan.
2. Stir in the milk or cream and chicken broth, or the 2 cups milk.
3. Cook, stirring, over moderate heat 3 to 4 minutes or until gravy has thickened.
4. Season to taste with salt and ground black pepper.

Yield: Approximately 1-3/4 cups.

SALADS

All salads should have eye appeal and should furnish their share of the nutrients needed by the body. A hearty salad may be the main dish for a luncheon or supper. A light salad may accompany the entrée or may be served as a separate course of a more formal meal.

Salad greens should be thoroughly washed, drained, dried, and served crackly-crisp. Tear, don't cut, the salad greens into bite-size pieces. Just before serving, toss them with oil, being sure that the oil coats every leaf so that the salad will not be watery. However, an excess of oil should be avoided. Do not toss tomatoes with other ingredients, since their juice makes the salad watery. Instead, arrange the pieces over the top of a tossed salad. Hearty salads, such as those made with potatoes and other cooked vegetables, macaroni, or rice, should be marinated in French dressing several hours or overnight to make them flavorsome. To retain the fresh look and texture, so appealing to the eye and palate, avoid unnecessary handling of salad ingredients.

APPLE COLE SLAW

1/2 cup sour cream
1/2 to 3/4 teaspoon dill seed
1/2 teaspoon salt
1 teaspoon lemon juice
1/16 teaspoon ground black
  pepper
1/2 teaspoon sugar

2 cups shredded raw cabbage
2 cups (2 medium-sized) diced
  unpeeled apples
lettuce
unpeeled diced apple for
  garnish

1. Combine the first 6 ingredients in a 1-1/2-quart mixing
  bowl.
2. Add cabbage and apples and mix lightly, but well.
3. Serve on lettuce and garnish with diced unpeeled apple.
Yield: 6 servings.

AVOCADO AND GRAPEFRUIT SALAD

romaine, washed, dried, and
  torn into bite-size pieces
grapefruit, peeled and cut into
  sections
avocado, peeled, sliced, and
  dipped into grapefruit juice

pimiento, cut into strips 1/8
  inch wide
Vinaigrette Salad Dressing

For each serving:

1. Put 1/2 cup romaine on an individual salad plate.
2. Arrange 3 grapefruit sections and three avocado slices over
  the romaine.

3. Garnish with 3 strips pimiento.
4. Serve with Vinaigrette Salad Dressing.

BLUEBERRY AND PINEAPPLE SALAD

1-1/2 cups raw pineapple wedges
1-1/2 cups raw blueberries
2 tablespoons French dressing (oil and vinegar type)

head lettuce
mayonnaise
cottage cheese

1. Combine the first 3 ingredients and arrange the mixture on lettuce leaves.
2. Serve with mayonnaise or cottage cheese and Cheese Pinwheels or Cheesy Fan Rolls.
Yield: 5 servings.

CABBAGE AND SPINACH SLAW

3 cups finely shredded cabbage
1-1/2 cups finely shredded raw spinach
1 tablespoon finely chopped onion

1/2 teaspoon salt
1/8 teaspoon ground black pepper

1/2 teaspoon dill seed
2 teaspoons lemon juice or cider vinegar
3 tablespoons mayonnaise

6 radish roses

1. Combine cabbage, spinach, and onion in a 2-quart mixing bowl.
2. Add the next 5 ingredients and mix lightly but well.
3. Turn into a salad bowl and garnish with radish roses.
Yield: 6 servings.

CABBAGE AND CARROT SLAW

In the preceding recipe, replace the spinach with 1-1/2 cups finely shredded raw carrots. Garnish with chopped parsley.

JELLIED RAW-CRANBERRY SALAD

1 package (3 ounces) orange-flavored gelatin
1 cup boiling water
3/4 cup sugar
3/4 cup cold water
1 tablespoon lemon juice
1/16 teaspoon salt

3 cups whole raw cranberries, coarsely chopped
1 cup finely chopped celery
1/3 cup chopped pecans
lettuce
mayonnaise (optional)

1. Put gelatin and boiling water in a 2-quart mixing bowl. Stir to dissolve gelatin.
2. Add sugar. Mix well.
3. Stir in the next 3 ingredients.
4. Place the bowl in a pan of ice water to chill until the mixture is about as thick as fresh egg whites.
5. Fold in cranberries, celery, and pecans.

6. Turn the mixture into a lightly oiled 9 x 9 x 2-inch pan, or into 6 lightly oiled individual molds.
7. Refrigerate salad until gelatin is firm and you are ready to serve it.
8. Serve on lettuce with mayonnaise, if desired.

Yield: 6 to 8 servings.

CRAB MEAT SALAD

2 cups chilled, cooked crab meat

1-1/2 cups diced celery
1 tablespoon lemon juice
1 tablespoon catsup
3 tablespoons mayonnaise

1 teaspoon salt or salt to taste
1/4 teaspoon ground black pepper
1 teaspoon finely chopped onion

lettuce

1. Flake crab meat and pick out and discard all cartilage.
2. Combine crab meat with the next 7 ingredients. Mix lightly.
3. Serve on lettuce for lunch or supper with sliced tomatoes, Deviled Eggs, and crisp, hot Onion French Bread.

Yield: 6 servings.

CUCUMBER, GREEN PEPPER, AND RADISH SALAD

1 large unpeeled cucumber, sliced thin
1/2 teaspoon salt
2 green peppers, sliced thin

1 cup whole radishes, sliced thin
3 tablespoons oil and vinegar French Dressing

1. Combine cucumbers and salt and let stand 30 minutes.
2. Drain the cucumbers and place them on the bottom of a platter.
3. Cover the cucumber slices with a layer each of sliced green peppers and sliced radishes.
4. Pour the French Dressing over all. Chill 15 minutes.

Yield: 6 servings.

CUCUMBER FRUIT SALAD

2 medium-sized Bartlett pears, peeled and cored
1 tablespoon lemon juice
1 tablespoon mayonnaise
1 tablespoon sour cream
1 cup orange sections or mandarin oranges, drained
1 cup green seedless grapes
lettuce
1 medium-sized cucumber, unpeeled

1. Cut pears into lengthwise slices 3/8 inch thick and dip them into lemon juice to prevent discoloration.
2. Mix mayonnaise with sour cream and add.
3. Add the next 2 ingredients and mix lightly.
4. Place the salad mixture on lettuce.
5. Score unpeeled cucumber by running a fork down the side of the cucumber. Cut cucumber into thin crosswise slices and insert slices at intervals over the salad.
6. Serve with toasted cheese sandwiches, ham sandwiches, or chicken salad sandwiches.

Yield: 6 servings.

HEARTY FALL SALAD

1 cup canned kidney beans, well drained

1 cup canned whole-kernel corn, well drained

1/2 cup diced celery

3/4 teaspoon salt or salt to taste

1-1/2 to 2 teaspoons chili powder

3 tablespoons mayonnaise

lettuce or other salad greens

3/4 cup coarsely diced tomatoes

1. Combine the first 6 ingredients in a 2-quart mixing bowl and toss lightly but thoroughly.
2. Line a salad bowl with lettuce or other salad greens.
3. Turn salad into the bowl and sprinkle diced tomatoes over the top.
4. Serve for lunch or supper with cold baked ham, cold roast beef or cold roast veal, and hot Cornbread or hot All-Purpose Rolls.

Yield: 6 servings.

MOLDED ORANGE AND CARROT SALAD

1 package (3 ounces) orange-flavored gelatin

1 cup boiling water

1 cup orange juice

1 tablespoon lemon juice

1 cup grated carrots

lettuce or watercress

mayonnaise

1. Put gelatin and boiling water in a 2-quart mixing bowl. Stir to dissolve gelatin.
2. Add orange juice and lemon juice.

3. Place the bowl in a pan of ice water to chill until the mixture is about as thick as fresh egg whites.
4. Fold in grated carrots.
5. Pour mixture into a lightly oiled 8 x 8 x 2-inch pan.
6. Refrigerate the salad until gelatin is firm and you are ready to serve it.
7. Cut salad into 8 squares and serve on lettuce or watercress. Top with mayonnaise.

Yield: 8 servings.

POLYNESIAN LOBSTER SALAD

A superbly elegant salad for a luncheon.

2 cups diced, cooked, cold lobster or 4 lobster tails, 5 ounces each

1-1/2 cups diced green celery
1-1/2 cups raw pineapple wedges
1 teaspoon salt

1/8 teaspoon ground black pepper
dash cayenne (optional)
2-1/2 teaspoons soy sauce or soy sauce to taste
1/3 cup mayonnaise
crisp lettuce

1. Cook lobster tails according to package directions.
2. Remove meat from shells, cut into dice, and cool.
3. Combine the cold lobster meat with the next 7 ingredients. Mix lightly, but well.
4. Serve on crisp lettuce with sliced cucumbers, clusters of grapes, and hot Cheese Biscuits with butter.

Yield: 6 servings.

MIXED GREEN SALAD
(INSALATA MISTA)

1/4 pound fresh young tender dandelion greens

1/4 head curly endive

1/4 head romaine lettuce

1/4 head iceberg or Boston lettuce

1 clove garlic, cut in half

1/2 cup shredded celery leaves

Anchovy Salad Dressing, Blue Cheese Salad Dressing, or Creamy French Dressing

1. Wash dandelion greens, endive, romaine lettuce, and iceberg or Boston lettuce, drain well, and wrap in a clean towel to dry thoroughly.
2. Rub the inside of a wooden salad bowl with garlic. Discard garlic.
3. Tear salad greens into bite-size pieces and put them into the salad bowl. Add celery leaves.
4. Just before serving, pour 1/4 cup Anchovy Salad Dressing (or as much as desired) over the greens and toss them lightly.
5. Serve promptly.

Yield: 6 servings.

SPAGHETTI AND CHEESE SALAD

3 cups cold, cooked spaghetti (spaghetti broken in 1-inch pieces before cooking)

1 cup diced cucumber

3 tablespoons chopped pimiento

1 cup finely shredded sharp Cheddar cheese

1/4 to 1/3 cup mayonnaise

salt to taste

lettuce or watercress

radish roses

1. Put the first 4 ingredients in a 2-quart mixing bowl.
2. Add enough mayonnaise to moisten the mixture, salt to taste, and toss lightly.
3. Serve on lettuce or watercress, and garnish each serving with a radish rose.
4. Serve for lunch or supper with cold sliced meat and sliced tomatoes.

Yield: 6 generous servings.

SESAME-SEED APPLE AND CARROT SALAD

2-1/2 cups diced unpeeled apples
1 cup shredded raw carrots
1/2 cup diced celery
3 tablespoons mayonnaise
3 tablespoons Toasted Sesame Seed (see following recipe)
lettuce

1. Combine the first 4 ingredients with 2 tablespoons toasted sesame seed. Toss lightly and serve on lettuce.
2. Sprinkle 1/2 teaspoon toasted sesame seed over each serving.

Yield: 6 servings.

TO TOAST SESAME SEED

Put sesame seed in a shallow baking pan and heat in a preheated moderate oven (350°F.) 20 to 22 minutes or until seeds are golden brown. Stir a couple of times to toast seeds uniformly.

PEAR WALDORF SALAD

3 cups diced ripe pears (about 3 large pears)

1 tablespoon lemon juice
_____

1 cup diced celery

1/2 cup chopped pecans or walnuts

2 tablespoons mayonnaise
_____

lettuce

1. Dice pears into lemon juice to prevent discoloration.
2. Add the next 3 ingredients and mix lightly.
3. Serve on lettuce and if desired, sprinkle with additional chopped pecans or walnuts.

Yield: 6 servings.

APPLE WALDORF SALAD

In the preceding recipe, replace diced pears with 3 cups diced ripe, unpeeled apples.

TOSSED GRAPE AND CABBAGE SALAD

3 cups shredded raw green cabbage or red cabbage

1 cup green seedless grapes, or seeded Tokay or Malaga grapes

salt and ground black pepper to taste

1/4 to 1/3 cup Cucumber Mayonnaise
_____

lettuce

clusters of green grapes for garnish

1. Put the first 4 ingredients in a 2-quart mixing bowl. Toss lightly but thoroughly.

2. Serve on lettuce. Garnish with clusters of grapes.
Yield: 6 servings.

TOSSED ORANGE AND ONION SALAD

1 small clove garlic, split
3 tablespoons salad oil
1-1/2 quarts mixed salad greens (lettuce, romaine, and curly endive)
2 medium-sized navel oranges, peeled and cut into crosswise slices

1/2 cup small white onion rings

2 tablespoons lemon juice
3/4 teaspoon sugar
1/4 teaspoon salt
1/2 teaspoon powdered mustard soaked in 1 teaspoon water

1. Soak garlic in oil for 1 hour.
2. Tear salad greens into bite-size pieces, and put them in a salad bowl.
3. Remove garlic from oil, pour the oil over the greens, and toss them lightly but well.
4. Arrange orange slices and onion rings over greens.
5. Just before serving, combine the remaining 4 ingredients, pour mixture over salad, and toss lightly.
6. Serve promptly.
Yield: 6 generous servings.

TOSSED GRAPEFRUIT AND ONION SALAD

In the recipe for Tossed Orange and Onion Salad replace the oranges with sections from 1 medium-sized grapefruit. Proceed according to directions in the recipe.
Yield: 6 generous servings.

SHRIMP AND CANTALOUPE SALAD

A good salad for a warm-weather luncheon.

2 cups cooked shrimp, peeled and deveined

1 cup chopped celery
1/2 teaspoon salt
1/8 teaspoon ground black pepper

1 tablespoon lemon juice
1/4 cup mayonnaise

3 small cantaloupes
6 small sprigs watercress or parsley

1. Reserve 6 of the biggest and prettiest shrimp for use as a garnish.
2. Combine the remaining shrimp with the next 5 ingredients. Mix lightly, but well. Chill.
3. Shortly before serving, cut cantaloupe into crosswise halves, remove the seeds, and drain the cantaloupe.
4. Fill halves with the shrimp salad mixture and garnish with a sprig of watercress or parsley and 1 whole shrimp.

Yield: 6 servings.

ORIENTAL SHRIMP SALAD

2 cups diced celery
2 cups (1 pound can) bean sprouts, well drained
2 cans (4-1/2 ounces each) wet pack shrimp, well drained
2-1/2 teaspoons soy sauce

4 tablespoons mayonnaise
salt to taste
1/4 teaspoon ground black pepper

lettuce
paprika

1. Put the first 7 ingredients in a 2-quart mixing bowl and toss lightly.
2. Serve on lettuce and garnish with paprika.

Yield: 6 servings.

TUNA FISH AND SPINACH SALAD

1 can (6-1/2 ounces) tuna fish, flaked

1/2 cup diced celery

1-1/2 cups chopped, raw, tender spinach leaves

1/2 teaspoon instant minced onion or 2 teaspoons chopped raw onion

1/2 teaspoon salt or salt to taste

1/16 teaspoon ground black pepper

2 tablespoons French Dressing

2 tablespoons mayonnaise

2 tomatoes, cut into 8 wedges

1. Put all ingredients, except tomato wedges, in a 2-quart mixing bowl and toss lightly.
2. Serve for lunch or supper garnished with tomato wedges.

Yield: 4 servings.

SALAD DRESSINGS

ANCHOVY SALAD DRESSING

2 tablespoons lemon juice

3 tablespoons olive oil or salad oil

1 tablespoon chopped parsley

1 tablespoon capers

2 teaspoons grated onion

3 flat anchovy fillets, chopped

1/2 teaspoon salt

1/8 teaspoon ground black pepper

Put all ingredients in a small mixing bowl and beat with a rotary beater 1/2 minute.
Yield: 1/2 cup dressing.

AVOCADO MAYONNAISE

A delightfully different dressing for seafood salads or vegetable salads.

1 medium-small avocado   1/4 teaspoon grated onion
1 to 2 teaspoons lemon juice   1/2 cup mayonnaise
  (lemon juice to taste)

1. Wash the avocado, wipe dry, cut in half, peel and remove the seed.
2. Dice avocado into lemon juice to prevent discoloration.
3. Mash the avocado and put it through a sieve, or purée it in an electric blender.
4. Stir in the grated onion and mayonnaise.
Yield: 1 cup.

CUCUMBER MAYONNAISE

Serve over vegetable or seafood salads and over baked or broiled fish. Make shortly before using to prevent the cucumbers from becoming watery.

1/2 cup diced unpeeled cu-   1/2 cup mayonnaise
  cumbers

1. Blend cucumbers with mayonnaise.
2. Add to vegetable or seafood salad and mix well, but lightly.
3. Serve at once.
Yield: 2/3 cup.

FRUIT SALAD DRESSING

2 packages (3 ounces each) cream cheese, softened

2 teaspoons sugar

1/16 teaspoon salt or salt to taste

1/3 cup orange juice

1. Mix cream cheese with salt and sugar.
2. Gradually blend in orange juice. Mix until fluffy.
3. Serve over fruit salads.
Yield: 1 cup dressing.

BLUE CHEESE SALAD DRESSING

1/3 cup mayonnaise

1/4 cup sour cream

1 tablespoon lemon juice

1/4 cup crumbled blue cheese

Combine all ingredients. Serve with fruit salads.
Yield: A generous 3/4 cup.

CRANBERRY WHIPPED-CREAM
SALAD DRESSING

1/3 cup strained cranberry sauce

1/2 cup mayonnaise

1/2 cup heavy cream, whipped

1. Combine cranberry sauce and mayonnaise. Fold in whipped cream.
2. Serve over fruit salads.

Yield: 1-3/4 cups.

FRENCH DRESSING

(OIL AND VINEGAR TYPE)

1 clove garlic
3/4 cup salad oil
1/4 cup cider vinegar or tarragon vinegar
1 teaspoon salt
1/2 teaspoon powdered mustard soaked in 1 teaspoon water
1/4 teaspoon ground black pepper
2 teaspoons grated onion
1 tablespoon sugar or honey

1. Soak garlic in oil 1 hour.
2. Remove garlic and discard. Add remaining 6 ingredients.
3. Beat well with a rotary beater or wire whisk.

Yield: 1 generous cup.

VINAIGRETTE SALAD DRESSING

1 small clove garlic
3/4 cup salad oil or olive oil
3/4 teaspoon salt
1 tablespoon sugar
1 tablespoon chopped green pepper
1 tablespoon pickle relish
1 teaspoon chopped capers
2 teaspoons chopped chives or chopped white onion
1/4 cup wine vinegar or cider vinegar

1. Soak garlic in oil 1 hour.
2. Remove and discard garlic. Add remaining 7 ingredients to the oil, and mix well.

Yield: Approximately 1 cup.

CREAMY FRENCH DRESSING

1 clove garlic
1 cup salad oil

1 teaspoon salt
1/2 teaspoon powdered mustard soaked in 1 teaspoon water
1/8 teaspoon ground black pepper

1 teaspoon grated onion
2 tablespoons catsup
2 tablespoons honey or un-sulphured molasses
1/3 cup cider vinegar
1 medium-sized egg white

1. Soak garlic in oil 1 hour. Remove and discard garlic.
2. Add remaining 8 ingredients and beat vigorously with a rotary beater.

Yield: Approximately 1-1/2 cups.

SANDWICHES

Sandwiches are versatile in that they fit into the scheme of many types of meals — from the dainty bite-size appetizers and party sandwiches to the hearty lunch-box and main-dish sandwiches. Here are a few tips for making sandwiches:

Use fine-textured day-old bread.

Have the spreads at a fairly soft spreading consistency. Spread one side of each slice of bread with softened butter or margarine. Spread it lightly but out to the very edges of the bread. This prevents the filling from soaking into the bread. Spread the filling generously, but not so lavishly that it oozes out. A flexible spatula is a suitable tool.

Leave crusts on the bread for all sandwiches except dainty appetizer or party sandwiches. The crusts aid in keeping sandwiches fresh.

Cut sandwiches into halves, thirds, or fourths. Unless they are to be eaten immediately, wrap them in waxed paper, plastic wrap, or foil.

Sandwiches for lunch boxes or picnic baskets should be wrapped and frozen. They will be thawed and fresh-tasting when they are served.

BEEF AND CABBAGE SANDWICHES

1-3/4 cups ground cooked beef
1 tablespoon finely chopped
   onion
1 tablespoon catsup
2 tablespoons mayonnaise
salt and ground black pepper
   to taste

12 slices firm-textured sandwich bread, buttered on 1
   side
about 1-1/2 cups finely shredded raw cabbage

1. Put the first 5 ingredients in a 1-1/2-quart mixing bowl and mix well.
2. Spread the filling on the buttered side of 6 bread slices.
3. Top the filling of each with about 1/4 cup shredded cabbage.
4. Cover each with remaining buttered bread slice, having the buttered side next to the cabbage.

Yield: 6 sandwiches.

GRILLED OPEN-FACE CRAB MEAT SANDWICHES

3 hard-cooked eggs
1 can (6-1/2 ounces) crab
   meat, flaked
salt and ground black pepper
1/4 teaspoon powdered mustard soaked in 1 teaspoon
   water

1 tablespoon lemon juice
3 tablespoons mayonnaise
6 slices firm-textured bread
6 slices tomato
melted butter or margarine

1. Peel eggs, chop all the whites, and 2 of the yolks. (Reserve the remaining yolk to use later.)
2. Combine crab meat, 3/4 teaspoon salt, 1/4 teaspoon black pepper, chopped eggs, and the next 3 ingredients.
3. Spread the mixture over the bread slices.
4. Top each sandwich with a slice of tomato, and brush it with melted butter or margarine. Sprinkle with salt and black pepper to taste.
5. Broil in the oven broiler 5 to 8 minutes.
6. Put the remaining egg yolk through a sieve, and sprinkle sieved yolk over the tomatoes. Serve hot.

Oven broiler temperature: 550°F. (broil).

Broiling time: 5 to 8 minutes.

Yield: 3 servings.

FLOWER POT SANDWICHES

unsliced white bread or whole-wheat bread

fillings (see following recipes)
parsley

1. Cut bread into slices about 1 inch thick, then cut slices into rounds with a round 1-1/2 to 2-inch cooky cutter.
2. With kitchen scissors, cut out the centers of the rounds, leaving the sides and bottoms about 1/4 inch thick, simulating flower pots.
3. Fill centers with one or more of the fillings.
4. Insert a small sprig of parsley in the top of each filled flower pot.

Allow 2 to 3 sandwiches per person.

FILLINGS

EGG SALAD FILLING

4 hard-cooked eggs, peeled and chopped fine

1/3 cup finely chopped celery

1 tablespoon finely chopped green pepper

1/4 teaspoon instant minced onion or 1 teaspoon chopped raw onion

1 tablespoon pickle relish

3 tablespoons mayonnaise or enough to moisten the mixture

salt and ground black pepper to taste

1. Combine all ingredients and spoon the filling into the centers of the bread flower pots.

Yield: Filling for approximately 30 flower pots.

CHICKEN SALAD FILLING

1 cup finely chopped, cold, cooked chicken

1/3 cup finely chopped celery

1/4 teaspoon lemon juice

2 to 3 tablespoons mayonnaise

salt and ground black pepper to taste

1. Mix the first 3 ingredients with enough mayonnaise to moisten the mixture.
2. Add salt and pepper to taste, and spoon the mixture into the centers of the bread flower pots.

Yield: 1 generous cup filling, or enough filling for approximately 16 flower pots.

TUNA FISH SALAD FILLING

In the preceding recipe for Chicken Salad Filling, replace the 1 cup chicken with 1 can (6-1/2 ounces) tuna fish. Continue according to directions in the recipe.

Yield: Filling for approximately 12 flower pots.

TURKEY SANDWICHES WITH HOT CHEESE SAUCE

2 tablespoons butter or margarine

2 tablespoons flour

3/4 turkey broth
1/2 cup milk
1/4 teaspoon poultry seasoning

1/2 cup shredded mild American cheese
cold sliced turkey
8 slices firm-textured bread
snipped parsley

1. Melt butter or margarine in a 1-quart saucepan.
2. Blend in flour. Stir and cook 1 minute or until the mixture foams.
3. Stir in the next 3 ingredients and cook, stirring, until the sauce is of medium thickness.
4. Remove sauce from heat and add cheese.
5. Place cold sliced turkey on bread slices (2 slices per serving) and spoon 1/4 cup cheese sauce over each serving.
6. Garnish with snipped parsley and serve with a fruit salad, or Molded Cranberry Salad.

Yield: 4 servings.

OPEN-FACE CHEESE AND ONION SANDWICHES

1/2 pound sharp Cheddar
cheese

1 medium-sized Bermuda
onion

dash cayenne

1/8 teaspoon salt

1/8 teaspoon ground black
pepper

4 strips crisp bacon, crumbled

8 slices firm-textured sandwich bread

chopped parsley

1. Put the cheese and onion through a food chopper, using the medium blade, or chop the cheese and onion fine.
2. Add the next 4 ingredients and mix well.
3. Toast the bread on one side in the broiler oven.
4. Spread untoasted side of bread with the cheese mixture.
5. Place the sandwiches on a cooky sheet and put them in the broiler oven to melt the cheese.
6. Sprinkle with chopped parsley and serve promptly for lunch or supper with sliced tomatoes and watercress or lettuce.

Yield: 4 servings, 2 sandwiches each.

OPEN-FACE EGG-AND-CAVIAR PARTY SANDWICHES

A good way to stretch the caviar and add glamour to the sandwich tray.

2-1/2-inch circles firm-textured bread

butter, softened

snipped parsley

hard-cooked eggs, sliced crosswise 1/8 inch thick

black or red caviar

1. Spread each round of bread on 1 side with softened butter.
2. Roll edges in snipped parsley.
3. Place a slice of hard-cooked egg in the center of each round of bread.
4. Top each with about 1/4 teaspoon black caviar or red caviar.

Yield: Allow 2 to 3 sandwiches per person.

OPEN-FACE HAM-AND-EGG PARTY SANDWICHES

In the recipe for Open-Face Egg and Caviar Party Sandwiches, replace the caviar on each sandwich with 1/2 teaspoon deviled ham. Garnish with a slice of pimiento-stuffed olive.
Yield: Allow 2 to 3 sandwiches per person.

HOT HAM AND CHEESE BUNS

1-1/2 cups (1/2 pound) diced spiced ham

3/4 cup diced sharp American cheese

3 tablespoons pickle relish

3 tablespoons mayonnaise

1 teaspoon prepared mustard

1/2 teaspoon celery salt

1/2 teaspoon onion salt

6 hamburger buns, buttered

1. Combine the first 7 ingredients and spoon the mixture into the hamburger buns.
2. Wrap each bun in foil and place them in a baking pan.

3. Heat in a preheated slow oven until buns are hot. Or if desired, heat the buns on the barbecue grill over slow-burning coals.

Oven temperature: 325°F. (slow).

Cooking time: Approximately 30 minutes.

Yield: 6 servings.

SAUCES

A perfect sauce is thoroughly blended, velvety smooth, and delicately seasoned. The sauces in this chapter are for meats, fish, shellfish, vegetables, and desserts.

COCKTAIL SAUCE

1/2 cup tomato catsup
2 teaspoons horseradish sauce
4 teaspoons lemon juice
1/2 teaspoon salt
3/4 teaspoon chili powder

1/8 teaspoon cayenne or cayenne to taste
1/16 teaspoon garlic powder or finely chopped fresh garlic

1. Combine all ingredients.
2. Chill, and serve with crab meat, lobster, oysters, or shrimp for the appetizer course.

Yield: Approximately 2/3 cup.

CURRY BUTTER SAUCE

1. Melt 2 tablespoons butter in a small saucepan.
2. Blend in 1 teaspoon curry powder.

3. Serve with cooked vegetables, fish, or shellfish.
Yield: 2 to 4 servings.

DILLY BUTTER SAUCE

In the recipe for Curry Butter Sauce, substitute 1 teaspoon dill seed for the curry powder. Cook, stirring, 1 to 2 minutes, until butter has browned. Serve with cooked vegetables, fish, or shellfish.
Yield: 2 to 4 servings.

HERBED LEMON BUTTER

1/4 cup (1/2 stick) butter or margarine, softened
1 tablespoon lemon juice or lemon juice to taste

1 teaspoon snipped fresh parsley, or 1/2 teaspoon snipped fresh chervil, fresh thyme, or fresh tarragon

1. Combine all ingredients. Mix until butter is fluffy.
2. Serve in small hearts of lettuce leaves as an accompaniment to fish and shellfish.
Yield: 1/3 cup butter.

CUCUMBER SAUCE FOR FISH

1 cup finely chopped peeled cucumbers
1/2 teaspoon salt
1 tablespoon sugar

1 tablespoon cider vinegar
1/8 teaspoon ground white pepper
1/2 cup heavy cream, whipped

1. Put cucumber and salt in a small bowl and mix well.
2. Cover and refrigerate 1 hour.
3. Drain the cucumbers well and squeeze out excess water.
4. Add the next 3 ingredients. Mix well.
5. Shortly before serving, fold in whipped cream.
6. Serve over baked salmon, halibut, swordfish, or haddock.

Yield: A generous 1 cup.

FRESH CRANBERRY SAUCE

There is no need to search for a recipe for cranberry sauce if this easy rule of thumb is remembered – 4 – 2 – 1: 4 cups raw cranberries, 2 cups sugar, and 1 cup water.

1 pound (4 cups) raw cran-   2 cups sugar
  berries, washed   1 cup water

1. Put all the ingredients in a 2-quart saucepan. Cook, covered, until cranberry skins break, 8 to 10 minutes. If cranberries are overcooked, the sauce will be bitter.
2. Remove sauce from heat and cool.
3. Serve with all meats and poultry.

Yield: Approximately 3-1/2 cups.

JELLY AND ORANGE SAUCE

1 cup (8-ounce glass) currant,   3/4 cup diced orange sections
  apple, or guava jelly

1. Break up the jelly with a fork.
2. Add diced oranges and gently fold into the jelly.
3. Serve with ham, pork, duck, or goose.

Yield: 1-3/4 cups.

MUSTARD SAUCE

1 tablespoon flour
2 tablespoons sugar
1/4 teaspoon salt
_____
1 large egg
2 teaspoons powdered mus-
tard soaked in 2 teaspoons
water
1 cup milk
2 tablespoons lemon juice or
vinegar

1. Mix first 3 ingredients in the top of a double boiler.
2. Beat in egg. Stir in mustard and milk.
3. Cook, covered, over hot water (not boiling) until the sauce
   has thickened, 5 to 8 minutes, stirring frequently.
4. Add lemon juice or vinegar.
5. Serve over ham, beef, or fish.

Yield: 1-1/4 cups.

ORANGE SAUCE FOR HAM

1/4 cup ham fat
2 tablespoons flour
_____
1/3 cup water
1 cup orange juice
1/4 cup sugar
1/3 cup seedless raisins
2 teaspoons grated fresh
orange rind
1 teaspoon grated fresh lemon
rind

1. Melt ham fat in a 1-quart saucepan. Blend in flour.
2. Gradually stir in next 3 ingredients. Stir and cook over medium heat until the sauce begins to thicken.
3. Add raisins and cook 3 to 4 minutes longer.
4. Remove from heat and stir in grated orange rind and lemon rind.
5. Serve over baked or boiled ham.

Yield: 1-1/2 cups.

SPANISH SAUCE

3 tablespoons olive oil or salad oil

2/3 cup finely chopped onion

1/3 cup finely chopped celery

1/3 cup finely chopped sweet green pepper

2 cups (1 pound, 3 ounces) canned tomatoes, strained

1/4 teaspoon sugar

1-1/2 teaspoons salt or salt to taste

1/2 to 1 teaspoon ground black pepper

1. Heat oil in a 1-quart saucepan. Add onion and cook 3 to 4 minutes or until onion is soft.
2. Stir in the remaining 6 ingredients. Simmer, uncovered, 1/2 hour or until sauce has thickened, stirring frequently.
3. Serve over meat loaf, meat patties, ham, pork, tongue, omelets, or poached eggs.

Yield: 2 cups.

FOUNDATION WHITE SAUCE

2 tablespoons butter or margarine
2 tablespoons flour
1 cup milk, heated

1/2 teaspoon salt
1/8 teaspoon ground black pepper

1. Melt butter or margarine in a 1-quart saucepan.
2. Remove saucepan from heat and blend in flour.
3. Cook, stirring, over low heat until mixture is bubbly.
4. Remove saucepan from heat and beat in hot milk. Continue beating until sauce is smooth.
5. Cook, stirring, about 1 minute over medium-low heat.
6. Add salt and pepper.
7. Use for sauces for creamed seafood, meats, poultry, and vegetables.

Yield: 1 cup.

VARIATIONS:

CAPER SAUCE

Add 2 tablespoons chopped capers to 1 cup White Sauce. Serve with fish.

CAPER-CHEESE SAUCE

Add 3/4 cup finely shredded Cheddar cheese and 2 tablespoons chopped capers to 1 cup White Sauce. Serve with fish and vegetables from the cabbage family.

CREAM SAUCE

In the preceding recipe for White Sauce, replace milk with 1 cup light cream. Serve with eggs, fish and shellfish, chicken or turkey, and vegetable dishes.

CREAMED HORSERADISH SAUCE

Add 2 tablespoons prepared horseradish to 1 cup White Sauce. Serve over meats and vegetables.

EGG SAUCE

Add 2 diced hard-cooked eggs, 2 teaspoons lemon juice, and 1/4 teaspoon powdered mustard soaked in 1/2 teaspoon water to 1 cup White Sauce. Serve over fish dishes and vegetables.

VELOUTÉ SAUCE

In the recipe for White Sauce, replace milk with 1 cup chicken broth, veal stock, or fish stock. Serve over croquettes, baked or broiled fish, and vegetables.

BLENDER HOLLANDAISE SAUCE

3 large egg yolks or 2 whole
   large eggs
2 tablespoons lemon juice
1/4 teaspoon salt or salt to
   taste

dash cayenne

1/2 cup (1 stick) butter or margarine, melted but not browned

1. Put the first 4 ingredients in the blender container. Cover, and blend about 1 minute or until the ingredients are blended.
2. Remove cover of container jar, turn on motor, and gradually pour in hot melted butter. Turn off motor.
3. Serve promptly, or if sauce must wait before serving, put it in a jar, and place the jar in a pan of hot water (not boiling) to keep warm.
4. Serve over vegetables, fish, and shellfish.

Yield: Approximately 3/4 cup.

BÉARNAISE SAUCE

1 recipe Blender Hollandaise Sauce
1 teaspoon onion juice
1 tablespoon tarragon vinegar
1 teaspoon chopped fresh tarragon or 1/4 teaspoon dried tarragon leaves, crumbled

Combine all ingredients and serve with baked, broiled, or poached fish, steak, or asparagus.

Yield: Approximately 3/4 cup.

TARTARE SAUCE

1 cup mayonnaise
1 tablespoon chopped capers
1 tablespoon chopped green olives
1 tablespoon chopped mixed sweet pickle
1 tablespoon chopped parsley
1/2 teaspoon paprika (optional)

Combine all ingredients, and serve with fish or use as a dressing for fish and shellfish salads.
Yield: 1-1/4 cups.

DESSERT SAUCES

CHOCOLATE SAUCE

A delicious smooth sauce that is easy to make.

1 tablespoon butter or margarine

2 squares (2 ounces) unsweetened chocolate

1 cup sugar

1-1/2 teaspoons cornstarch

1/8 teaspoon salt

3/4 cup boiling water

1 teaspoon vanilla extract

1. Melt butter or margarine and chocolate in the top of a 1-quart double boiler over hot water (not boiling).
2. Combine the next 3 ingredients and blend mixture with the melted butter and chocolate.
3. Stir in boiling water. Bring mixture to boiling point over direct surface heat. Boil 3 to 4 minutes, stirring often.
4. Cool. Stir in vanilla extract.
5. Serve over cake, ice cream, and other desserts.
Yield: 1-1/4 cups.

CHOCOLATE MINT SAUCE

Use the recipe for Chocolate Sauce and stir in 1/4 cup crushed after-dinner mints along with the boiling water. Cook as directed.

Then beat with a wire whisk until sauce is smooth. Increase vanilla extract to 1-1/2 teaspoons.

Yield: Approximately 1-1/2 cups.

EASY CHOCOLATE SAUCE

1 can (15-ounce) sweetened condensed milk

6-ounce package semi-sweet chocolate pieces

1/2 cup hot water

1 teaspoon vanilla extract

1. Put condensed milk and chocolate pieces in the top of a 1-quart double boiler.
2. Cook over hot water until chocolate is melted and is thoroughly blended with condensed milk.
3. Add the hot water and vanilla extract. Mix well.
4. Cool and serve over ice cream, plain cake, sponge cake, and puddings.

Yield: 2-1/4 cups.

FOAMY SAUCE

1-1/3 cups sifted confectioners' sugar

1/2 cup (1 stick) butter or margarine, softened

dash of salt

1 large egg, separated

2 tablespoons apricot or peach brandy or rum

1/2 cup heavy cream, whipped

ground nutmeg

1. Gradually blend confectioners' sugar into softened butter or margarine in the top of a double boiler.

2. Add salt and egg yolk. Mix well.
3. Place over hot water (not boiling) until mixture is light and fluffy, stirring frequently, 6 to 7 minutes.
4. Remove from heat, and stir in brandy or rum.
5. Beat egg white until it stands in soft, stiff peaks when beater is raised and fold it into the cooked mixture.
6. Fold in whipped cream and nutmeg just before serving.
7. Serve with steamed puddings or other desserts.

Yield: Approximately 2 cups.

HOT MAPLE SYRUP SAUCE

1-1/4 cups light brown sugar, firmly packed

3/4 cup maple syrup

1/4 cup (1/2 stick) butter or margarine

2/3 cup sweetened condensed milk

2 teaspoons vanilla extract

1. Combine the first 3 ingredients in a 1-quart saucepan. Cook slowly 5 minutes, stirring constantly.
2. Remove from heat. Add condensed milk and vanilla extract. Mix well.
3. Serve over ice cream, plain cake, or to make ice cream sodas.

Yield: 2-1/3 cups.

PRALINE CUSTARD SAUCE

4 tablespoons sugar

2 teaspoons cornstarch

1/16 teaspoon salt

2 large eggs, separated

1 cup light cream or milk

1/4 cup crumbled pralines

1. Combine 2 tablespoons of the sugar with cornstarch and salt in the top of a double boiler.
2. Blend in egg yolks. Gradually stir in cream or milk.
3. Cook, uncovered, over hot water (not boiling) until the mixture coats a metal spoon, stirring frequently.
4. Beat egg whites until they stand in soft, stiff peaks. Gradually beat in remaining 2 tablespoons sugar.
5. Fold hot custard into beaten egg whites. Then fold in pralines.
6. Serve over baked apples or pears, or cottage pudding.

Yield: 2 generous cups.

FRESH PEACH SAUCE

1 cup mashed fresh peaches
1 teaspoon lemon juice
1/4 cup sugar
1/4 teaspoon vanilla extract

1. Combine all ingredients. Mix well. Chill.
2. Serve over ice cream, plain cake, sponge cake, or gingerbread.

Yield: 1 cup.

PINEAPPLE SAUCE

1 tablespoon sugar
1 tablespoon cornstarch
1/16 teaspoon salt
1 cup (8-3/4-ounce can) crushed pineapple
1 tablespoon butter or margarine
1/4 teaspoon grated lemon rind
3/4 teaspoon vanilla extract

1. Combine the first 3 ingredients in a 1-quart saucepan. Mix well.
2. Blend in crushed pineapple.
3. Cook over medium heat, stirring constantly, until sauce has thickened, about 5 minutes.
4. Remove from heat. Stir in remaining 3 ingredients.
5. Cool. Serve over plain cake or sponge cake.

Yield: About 1 cup.

ORANGE DESSERT SAUCE

1/4 cup sugar
2 tablespoons flour
1/16 teaspoon salt
1 cup orange juice
___
1 tablespoon lemon juice

2 tablespoons butter or margarine
1/2 teaspoon grated orange rind
1/4 teaspoon vanilla extract

1. Put sugar, flour, and salt in a 3-cup saucepan and mix well.
2. Stir in orange juice.
3. Cook, stirring, until sauce has thickened, about 2 minutes.
4. Remove saucepan from heat and stir in the remaining 4 ingredients. Mix until all ingredients are blended.

Yield: Approximately 1-1/4 cups.

RELISHES

SPICED FIGS

1 can or jar (1 pound, 14 ounces) figs

1/2 cup sugar
1/4 cup cider vinegar
1/8 teaspoon salt

2 sticks cinnamon, each 2 inches long
1/4 teaspoon whole allspice, tied in a bag
whole cloves

1. Drain syrup from figs into a 2-quart saucepan.
2. Add the next 5 ingredients to syrup and mix well.
3. Bring the mixture to a full rolling boil and continue boiling 5 minutes.
4. Stick 2 whole cloves into each fig and add them to the hot spiced syrup.
5. Simmer, uncovered, 5 minutes (do not boil).
6. Remove and discard the spice bag.
7. Cool. Cover and chill for at least 24 hours before serving. Serve with all meats and poultry.

Yield: 18 to 24 spiced figs.

SPICED PEACHES OR PEARS

In the recipe for Spiced Figs, replace figs with 1 can (1 pound, 13 ounces) peach halves or pear halves. Proceed according to directions in the recipe.

Yield: 5 to 7 peach halves or pear halves.

BROILED PEACHES

6 large canned peach halves   ground cloves
6 teaspoons butter or margarine   3 tablespoons peach syrup

1. Arrange peach halves in an 8- or 9-inch pie plate, cut side up.
2. Put 1 teaspoon butter or margarine and a dash of cloves in the cavity of each.
3. Pour syrup into the pie plate around peaches.
4. Broil in oven broiler until peaches have browned lightly.
Broiler oven temperature: Set to BROIL.
Broiling time: 10 minutes.
Yield: 6 servings.

RAW CRANBERRY RELISH

1 medium-sized navel orange   3/4 cup sugar
2 cups raw cranberries   dash of salt

1. Grate yellow portion from orange rind and set aside.
2. Cut off and discard bitter white portion of the rind and put the rest of the orange and the cranberries through a food chopper, using the medium blade.
3. Add grated orange rind, sugar, and salt. Mix well.
4. Let stand at least 3 hours to give the flavors time to blend.
5. Serve with poultry, beef, ham, pork, and veal.
6. Store unused portion in a covered jar in the refrigerator. This relish will keep several weeks in the refrigerator.
Yield: About 2 cups.

SOUPS

The kind of soup to serve depends upon the type of meal and upon the weather.

Clear soup and consommé usually precede a dinner or luncheon at which a number of courses are served. Their purpose is to stimulate the appetite.

Light cream soups are appropriate for ladies' luncheons, especially on cool or cold days.

Bisques, chowders, soups heavy with meat or fish and vegetables, and hearty cream soups are usually served as the main dish for the family luncheon or supper, or for an informal meal with guests.

Jellied soups or fruit soups are usually featured in hot weather for lunch, supper, family dinner, or for more formal meals.

BLACK BEAN SOUP

1 can (10-1/2 ounces) condensed black bean soup
1 can (10-1/2 ounces) water
1/2 teaspoon chili powder
salt to taste

1 tablespoon lime juice or lemon juice

4 teaspoons sour cream
snipped parsley (optional)

1. Put the first 5 ingredients in a 1-1/2-quart saucepan and mix well.
2. Cook over surface heat only until soup is hot.
3. Serve promptly in soup bowls, each topped with 1 teaspoon sour cream. Garnish with snipped parsley if desired.

Yield: 4 servings, scant 3/4 cup each.

FISH CHOWDER

1/4 pound salt pork, sliced 1/8 inch thick

4 medium-sized onions, peeled and sliced 1/8 inch thick

2 cups boiling water

2 large potatoes, peeled and sliced 1/4 inch thick

2 pounds perch fillets or fillet of haddock

1-1/2 teaspoons salt or salt to taste

1/16 teaspoon instant minced garlic

2 cups milk

1/2 teaspoon ground black pepper

2 tablespoons butter or margarine

1/2 cup heavy cream (optional)

1. Fry salt pork until crisp in a Dutch oven or in a 4-quart soup kettle.
2. Remove the crisp pork slices from the kettle and set aside.
3. Cook onions in hot pork drippings until they are limp, 4 to 5 minutes.
4. Add water and potatoes. Cook, covered, until potatoes fall apart, about 20 minutes.

5. Add the next 4 ingredients. Simmer, covered, until fish falls apart, 5 to 6 minutes. (Do not boil the fish.)
6. Stir in black pepper, butter or margarine, and heavy cream, if used.
7. Serve in soup plates with crisp pork crumbled over each serving, with pilot crackers.

Yield: Approximately 6 servings.

GAZPACHO

A cold salad soup perfect for summer meals.

3-1/2 cups peeled, diced, fresh tomatoes
1-1/2 cups finely chopped green pepper
3/4 cup finely chopped onion
3 teaspoons salt or salt to taste.
3/4 teaspoon minced fresh garlic or 1/8 teaspoon instant minced garlic
1/4 teaspoon ground black pepper
1 tablespoon paprika
1/3 cup olive oil
2 cups cold water
1/2 cup lemon juice
1/2 cup thinly sliced unpeeled cucumber

1. Put the first 7 ingredients in a mixing bowl and gradually beat in olive oil.
2. Stir in water and lemon juice. Chill 3 to 4 hours.
3. Add cucumber slices just before serving.
4. Serve in soup bowls as the soup course.

Yield: 8 cups.

BUSY-DAY VICHYSSOISE

1 can (10-1/2 ounces) frozen condensed cream of potato soup

1 can (10-1/2 ounces) condensed onion soup

2 chicken bouillon cubes dissolved in 2 cups boiling water or 2 cups chicken broth

1 cup heavy cream

1/4 teaspoon ground white pepper

snipped parsley

snipped chives or snipped green onion tops

1. Put the first 4 ingredients in a 2-quart saucepan and mix well.
2. Heat only until hot and until flavors are blended. Add pepper.
3. Serve hot or cold sprinkled with snipped parsley and snipped chives or green onion tops.

Yield: 6 servings.

QUICK CLAM CHOWDER

1 can (10-1/2 ounces) beef broth

1/4 cup finely diced celery

1 cup diced potatoes

2 tablespoons minced green pepper

1 can (10-1/2 ounces) condensed beef-vegetable soup

2 cans (7 ounces each) minced clams

3/4 teaspoon poultry seasoning

1/2 teaspoon salt or salt to taste

ground black pepper

soda crackers or pilot crackers

1. Put the first 4 ingredients in a Dutch oven or soup kettle, cover and cook over low heat until vegetables are tender, 20 to 25 minutes.
2. Add the next 3 ingredients. Heat to boiling point.
3. Season with salt and black pepper to taste.
4. Put whole or crumbled soda crackers or pilot crackers in a soup bowl and add the hot soup. Serve promptly.

Yield: 6 servings.

OYSTER AND CORN CHOWDER

2-1/2 cups milk

1/4 cup finely chopped raw onion or 1 tablespoon instant minced onion

2 cups finely diced cooked potatoes

1 package (10 ounces) frozen whole-kernel corn or 1 can (12 ounces) whole-kernel corn

2 tablespoons butter or margarine

2 teaspoons salt or salt to taste

1/4 teaspoon ground black pepper

1 can (7 ounces) frozen soup oysters with liquor or 1 cup fresh soup oysters with liquor

soda crackers or pilot crackers

1. Put the first 7 ingredients in a 3-quart saucepan or soup kettle. Cook, covered, until very hot.
2. Stir in oysters and oyster liquor and simmer until oysters are plump and the edges begin to curl.
3. Serve with soda crackers or pilot crackers.

Yield: 6 servings.

LENTIL SOUP
(ZUPPA DI LENTICCHI)

1/2 pound dried lentils
salt
2 quarts water
3 tablespoons olive oil
1/4 cup finely chopped onion
1 clove of garlic, split in half
___
1/2 cup chopped celery

2 cups (16 ounces) canned tomatoes
1/2 teaspoon dried basil leaves
1/4 teaspoon ground black pepper
___
grated Romano cheese or grated Parmesan cheese

1. Wash lentils and cook with 1 teaspoon salt and the water according to package directions.
2. Heat oil in a 3-quart saucepan, add onions and garlic and cook over medium heat until onions are limp, 3 to 4 minutes.
3. Stir in the next 4 ingredients. Cook, covered, 10 minutes.
4. Add the cooked lentils and 3 teaspoons salt or salt to taste and heat 1 to 2 minutes. Remove and discard the garlic.
5. Serve hot in bowls. Sprinkle with grated cheese.

Yield: 2-1/2 quarts or 10 servings.

POTATO AND ONION SOUP AU GRATIN

4 medium-sized peeled potatoes, sliced 1/8 inch thick
1-1/2 cups onion rings
1 quart rich beef stock or 1-1/2 cans (10-1/2 ounces) beef bouillon and 1-1/2 cans water
1 teaspoon salt or salt to taste
___

2 tablespoons butter or margarine
1/2 cup milk or heavy cream
1/8 teaspoon ground black pepper
___
croutons
Swiss cheese, cut into slivers

1. Put the first 4 ingredients in a 2-quart saucepan and cook, covered, 20 minutes or until potatoes fall apart and onions are tender.
2. Remove saucepan from the heat and pour the mixture through a sieve into another 2-quart saucepan, pushing as much of the potatoes and onion through as possible.
3. Add the next 3 ingredients and cook *only* until the soup is hot, 3 to 4 minutes.
4. Serve as a main-dish soup with croutons and slivers of Swiss cheese.

Yield: 6 servings or 1-1/2 quarts.

QUICK VEGETABLE SOUP

1/2 tablespoon chopped beef suet or shortening

1 pound ground chuck

2 cans (10-1/2 ounces each) beef broth

2 soup cans hot water

1-1/2 teaspoons salt or salt to taste

1 cup diced raw carrots

1 cup diced celery

1 cup diced raw potatoes

1/2 cup diced raw onion or 2 tablespoons instant chopped onion

3-1/2 cups (1 pound 13 ounces) canned tomatoes

1/4 teaspoon ground black pepper

1. Put chopped suet or shortening and beef in a Dutch oven or in a heavy-bottom soup kettle.
2. Stir and cook over moderate heat until the meat loses its pink color.

3. Add the next 8 ingredients. Cover and cook 35 to 40 minutes or until the vegetables are tender.
4. Add black pepper and adjust the salt.
5. Serve hot as a main-dish soup.

Yield: Approximately 2 quarts or 8 servings, 1 cup each.

VEGETABLES

Methods for cooking vegetables in this chapter are: boiling, steaming, panning, and baking. They all observe the following two basic rules of cooking vegetables:

1. Cook vegetables in the minimum amount of water necessary to prevent scorching. The amount depends upon the size of the pan and the quantity of vegetables. Usually 1/4 to 1 inch of water in the pan is sufficient. Add more water if needed.
2. Cook vegetables *only* until crisp-tender. Do not overcook.

BEANS WITH MACARONI
(PASTA CON FAGIOLI)

1 cup dried navy beans

2-1/2 cups water

2 tablespoons olive oil or salad oil

1 clove of garlic, split

1/4 cup tomato sauce

1/4 cup sliced white onion

1-1/2 teaspoons dried oregano

1 teaspoon salt

1/4 teaspoon ground black pepper

2 tablespoons chopped parsley

1/2 pound elbow macaroni

grated Parmesan cheese

1. Wash beans and soak overnight in the water.
2. Put oil and garlic in a 2-quart saucepan and heat only until garlic begins to discolor. (Do not brown garlic.) Remove and discard garlic.
3. Add beans and water in which they were soaked and the next 6 ingredients. Simmer, covered, 2 to 2-1/2 hours or until beans are tender, adding additional water if necessary.
4. Meanwhile, cook macaroni according to package directions. Drain and add it to the cooked beans.
5. Toss the mixture lightly and sprinkle with grated Parmesan cheese.
6. Serve hot with Fresh Mushrooms with Onion Rings, buttered zucchini squash, Mixed Green Salad with Anchovy Salad Dressing, and Italian bread and butter.

Yield: 6 servings.

GREEN BEANS WITH TOMATO MAYONNAISE

May be served hot as a vegetable or chilled and served on a salad plate.

1 pound whole young tender green beans, tips removed
1 teaspoon salt
boiling water
Tomato Mayonnaise (see following recipe)

1. Put beans and salt in a 1-1/2-quart saucepan.
2. Pour in boiling water to a depth of 1 inch.
3. Bring water to boiling point and cook, uncovered, for 5 minutes.

4. Cover and continue cooking 10 to 12 minutes or *only* until beans are crisp-tender.
5. Drain water off beans and place a bundle of beans on each of 6 dinner plates.
6. Spoon ribbons of Tomato Mayonnaise across the center of each bundle.

Yield: 6 servings.

TOMATO MAYONNAISE

1/4 cup mayonnaise
2 tablespoons well-drained, finely diced, raw tomatoes
1 teaspoon lemon juice
1/4 teaspoon salt or salt to taste
dash ground black pepper

Combine all ingredients and serve over hot cooked vegetables or salads.

Yield: 1/3 cup.

GREEN BEANS AMANDINE

2 tablespoons butter
2 tablespoons sliced blanched almonds
2 packages (10 ounces each) frozen green beans or 1 pound fresh green beans, cooked

1. Melt butter in a small saucepan. Add almonds and heat, stirring, until butter has browned and almonds are straw color.

2. Add the sauce to hot, well-drained, cooked beans. Toss lightly.

Yield: 6 servings.

SCHNITZEL BEANS
(BEANS WITH TOMATOES)

1 pound green beans, washed and drained

4 strips bacon

1 cup chopped raw onion

2 cups diced raw tomatoes

1 teaspoon salt or salt to taste

1/8 teaspoon ground black pepper

1 cup boiling water

1. Remove tips from beans. Cut beans into 1-inch pieces.
2. Fry bacon very crisp, remove it from drippings, drain it well on paper towels, and set aside.
3. Cook onion in bacon drippings until soft, but not browned.
4. Add beans and all ingredients except bacon in a saucepan.
5. Simmer, covered, 30 to 40 minutes or until beans are tender. Serve hot topped with crumbled crisp bacon.

Yield: 6 servings.

GREEN BEANS WITH CELERY SAUCE

4 tablespoons (1/2 stick) butter or margarine

1 teaspoon finely chopped onion

1/4 cup finely diced celery hearts

salt and ground black pepper to taste

2 packages (10 ounces each) frozen green beans or 1 pound fresh green beans, cooked

1. Melt butter or margarine in a small saucepan.
2. Add onion and celery, and cook, stirring frequently, over low heat, until celery is tender and butter or margarine begins to brown, 4 to 5 minutes.
3. Drain all water from the cooked beans, add the celery sauce, salt and black pepper to taste.
4. Toss beans lightly but well to coat them with the sauce. Serve hot.

Yield: 6 servings.

LIMA BEANS WITH CHIVES AND SOUR CREAM

A most palatable combination.

2 packages (9 or 10 ounces each) frozen lima beans
1/2 cup sour cream
1-1/2 teaspoons salt
1/8 teaspoon ground white pepper
2 tablespoons snipped fresh chives

1. Cook lima beans according to package directions.
2. Drain beans, if necessary. Add sour cream, salt, white pepper, and 1 tablespoon of the snipped chives. Toss lightly, but well. Heat 1/2 minute.
3. Garnish with remaining 1 tablespoon snipped chives.

Yield: 6 servings.

HERBED BEETS

1-1/2 pounds (about 6 med-ium-sized) whole beets with 2 inches of the tops and the roots attached
boiling water

2 tablespoons butter or mar-garine, melted
1/2 teaspoon salt or salt to taste

1/2 teaspoon dried basil leaves (optional)
1/8 teaspoon ground black pepper
1 teaspoon lemon juice

snipped parsley or parsley flakes

1. Place washed whole beets in a 2-quart saucepan.
2. Add enough boiling water to cover beets completely.
3. Cook, covered, 35 to 40 minutes or until beets are tender.
4. Remove beets from heat, and drain off water.
5. Using the fingers, slip skins off the beets. Cut off and discard tops and roots. Slice beets 1/4 inch thick.
6. Combine the next 5 ingredients and pour over beets.
7. Toss lightly, and heat 3 to 4 minutes.
8. Serve hot, sprinkled with parsley or parsley flakes.
Yield: 6 servings.

BROCCOLI WITH SESAME-SEED BROWNED-BUTTER SAUCE

Broccoli is a strong-flavored vegetable which develops an even stronger flavor and a brownish color if overcooked. It should be cooked only until crisp-tender.

*2 pounds fresh broccoli
3/4 teaspoon salt
boiling water
6 tablespoons butter or margarine

2 tablespoons sesame seed
1/8 teaspoon ground black
pepper

1. Wash the broccoli, and trim off and discard the tough stem ends. Do not remove the tender stems since the whole tender stems are edible.
2. Split the large stems almost to the flowerets, or if the stems are very large, cut through the stems and the flowerets, making 2 pieces.
3. Place broccoli in a saucepan with salt. Pour in boiling water to a depth of 1 inch.
4. Bring water to boiling point and cook the broccoli, un-covered, 5 minutes.
5. Cover saucepan, and cook 10 to 15 minutes or until the broccoli is crisp-tender. Drain well.
6. Put butter or margarine and sesame seed in a small sauce-pan. Cook, stirring, 3 to 4 minutes, or until butter and sesame seed have browned. Add black pepper.
7. Pour the browned-butter sauce over each serving of cooked broccoli.

Yield: 6 servings.

*If desired, replace fresh broccoli with 2 10-ounce packages frozen broccoli, cooked according to package directions.

BROCCOLI WITH ANCHOVY SAUCE

3 tablespoons olive oil, butter, or margarine

6 flat anchovy fillets, chopped fine

1/8 teaspoon ground black pepper

1/2 teaspoon lemon juice

2 pounds broccoli, cooked (see preceding recipe)

1. Heat olive oil, butter, or margarine in a 9- or 10-inch skillet.
2. Stir in anchovies, black pepper, and lemon juice.
3. Add well-drained cooked broccoli and heat 3 minutes, turning once.
4. Serve hot with roast beef, roast pork, or roast veal, browned potatoes, Tossed Grapefruit and Onion Salad, and hot Onion French Bread.

Yield: 6 servings.

CABBAGE AMANDINE

1 head (2 pounds) cabbage

1 teaspoon salt

boiling water

6 tablespoons butter

1/3 cup slivered, blanched almonds

1 tablespoon lemon juice

1/16 teaspoon ground black pepper

1. Remove coarse outside leaves from cabbage and wash the head in cold water.
2. Cut head into 6 wedges. Cut out and discard core, and place wedges in a large saucepan.

3. Add salt, and pour in boiling water to a depth of 1 inch.
4. Bring water to boiling point and boil, uncovered, 5 minutes.
5. Cover saucepan and continue to cook until cabbage is crisp-tender, 12 to 15 minutes.
6. Drain off water and carefully transfer cabbage wedges to a platter.
7. Meanwhile, melt butter in a small saucepan, add almonds, and sauté them until butter and almonds are golden.
8. Add lemon juice and black pepper and pour over cabbage wedges. Serve promptly.

Yield: 6 servings.

BAKED CARROTS

10 medium-sized (1-1/2 pounds) carrots

2 teaspoons sugar
1 teaspoon salt
3/4 teaspoon ground ginger

1/16 teaspoon ground black pepper

1 tablespoon lemon juice

4 tablespoons (1/2 stick) butter or margarine

1. Peel carrots and cut them into crosswise slices 1/2 inch thick.
2. Butter a 1-1/2-quart casserole and spread carrots over the bottom.
3. Combine the next 5 ingredients and sprinkle over carrots.
4. Dot carrots with the butter or margarine.
5. Bake, covered, in a preheated oven until carrots are tender.

Oven temperature: 350°F. (moderate).

Baking time: 40 to 50 minutes.

Yield: 6 servings.

CARROTS WITH FRIED APPLES

2 large cooking apples (Rome Beauty, Jonathan, or McIntosh)

3 tablespoons butter or margarine

3 cups thinly sliced peeled carrots

1-1/2 teaspoons sugar

1/4 teaspoon salt

1. Wash and core unpeeled apples. Cut them into crosswise slices 1/4 inch thick.
2. Melt butter in a heavy-bottom 9- or 10-inch skillet.
3. Add apple slices and cook them over moderately low heat until they have browned on the under side.
4. Turn apples, add carrots, and sprinkle with sugar and salt.
5. Cover and cook over moderately low heat until carrots are crisp-tender. Serve hot with pork, ham, or chicken.

Yield: 6 servings.

LYONNAISE CARROTS

2 tablespoons butter or margarine

1/4 cup thin onion rings

3 cups thinly sliced young carrots

1 teaspoon sugar

1/4 teaspoon salt or salt to taste

dash ground black pepper

1. Melt butter or margarine in a heavy-bottom 1-1/2-quart saucepan.

2. Add the remaining 5 ingredients and simmer, covered, until carrots are tender, 8 to 10 minutes. Stir occasionally. Serve hot.
Yield: 5 servings.

CAULIFLOWER MIMOSA

1 medium-sized head cauliflower
1 teaspoon salt
boiling water

2 to 3 tablespoons mayonnaise
1 hard-cooked egg yolk, put
through a sieve

1. Remove coarse outer leaves from cauliflower, but leave a few of the tender inside leaves attached.
2. Cut out center core from the stalk end.
3. Wash cauliflower and place it, stalk end up, in a 3-quart saucepan. Add salt.
4. Add boiling water to a depth of 1 inch. Bring water to boiling point and cook, uncovered, 5 minutes.
5. Cover saucepan and cook the cauliflower 10 minutes longer.
6. Turn cauliflower head up in the water, and cook, covered, 15 minutes or until cauliflower is tender.
7. Transfer cauliflower to a round serving dish. Spread mayonnaise over the top, and sprinkle with sieved hard-cooked egg yolk.
Yield: 6 servings.

DILLY CUCUMBERS

1/3 cup sour cream
1 tablespoon cider vinegar
1 tablespoon water
1/2 teaspoon salt
1/8 teaspoon ground black
  pepper

finely chopped fresh dill
1 cup thinly sliced onion rings
2 cups thinly sliced unpeeled
  cucumbers

1. Put the first 5 ingredients in a small mixing bowl.
2. Add 2 tablespoons of the chopped fresh dill and mix well.
3. Add onion rings and cucumber slices, and toss lightly.
4. Turn the mixture into a shallow serving bowl, and sprinkle
   with chopped fresh dill.

Yield: 6 servings.

CURRIED CELERY AND APPLES

A delicious vegetable dish to serve with baked ham, roast pork,
  roast veal, and roast turkey.

3 cups diced celery
1/2 teaspoon salt
boiling water
3 tablespoons butter or margarine
1-1/2 cups diced baking apples
  (Rome Beauty, Jonathan,
  etc.)

1/4 cup onion rings
1-1/2 tablespoons flour
1-1/4 teaspoons curry powder
1/16 teaspoon ground black
  pepper

1. Place celery and salt in a 2-quart saucepan, and add boiling water to a depth of 1/2 inch.
2. Cover saucepan; bring water to boiling point. Cook 5 to 8 minutes or *only* until celery is crisp-tender.
3. Meanwhile, melt butter or margarine in a 9-inch skillet, add apples and onion rings, and cook, uncovered, 5 minutes or *only* until apples and onions are soft, but not mushy.
4. Carefully stir in flour, curry powder, and black pepper.
5. Drain water from cooked celery and add celery to the apple and onion mixture. Mix lightly. Cook 2 to 3 minutes.
6. Serve hot.

Yield: 6 servings.

EGGPLANT DRESSING

A popular dish in southeastern Texas and southern Louisiana.

1 medium-sized (1 pound) eggplant
1-1/2 teaspoons salt
boiling water
———
1-1/2 tablespoons instant minced onion or 1/3 cup chopped raw onion

1/16 teaspoon instant minced garlic or 1 small clove garlic, crushed
1/4 cup chopped green pepper
1 tablespoon bacon drippings
1/8 teaspoon ground black pepper
———
1-1/2 cups hot cooked rice

1. Wash eggplant and cut it into slices 3/4 inch thick.
2. Peel the slices, cut them into cubes, and put cubes in a 2-quart saucepan.

3. Add salt and boiling water to a depth of 1/2 inch.
4. Cover saucepan and bring water to boiling point. Continue cooking, over moderate heat, until eggplant is tender, 6 to 8 minutes, stirring occasionally.
5. Drain and discard water from the eggplant.
6. Stir in the next 5 ingredients and cook, stirring, 3 to 4 minutes.
7. Fold in rice just before serving.

Yield: 5 servings.

FRIED EGGPLANT, ITALIAN STYLE

3/4 cup olive oil or salad oil
1 large (1-1/2 pounds) egg-plant, peeled and cut into crosswise slices 1/2 inch thick

salt and ground black pepper to taste
6 tablespoons grated Parmesan cheese
chopped parsley

1. Heat 1/4 cup of the oil in a heavy-bottom 10-inch skillet.
2. Place as many slices of eggplant, in a single layer, in the hot oil as the skillet will accommodate.
3. Fry them until brown, turning to brown both sides, and adding more oil as needed. (Eggplant absorbs oil quickly.)
4. Arrange fried eggplant slices on a platter, sprinkle with salt and black pepper to taste, Parmesan cheese, and chopped parsley.
5. Serve promptly.

Yield: 6 servings.

FRESH MUSHROOMS AND ONION RINGS

1-1/2 pounds fresh mushrooms
3 tablespoons butter or margarine
1 cup onion rings
1 tablespoon water
3/4 teaspoon salt
1/8 teaspoon ground black pepper

1. Wash mushrooms and cut them into quarters if they are large, leave them whole if they are small. Set aside.
2. Melt 2 tablespoons of the butter or margarine in a 9- or 10-inch skillet, add onions and water, and cook them 3 to 4 minutes or until they are limp.
3. Add remaining butter or margarine and mushrooms.
4. Cook, covered, 6 to 8 minutes over medium-low heat.
5. Season with salt and black pepper. Serve promptly.
Yield: 6 servings.

BAKED ONIONS

8 whole medium-sized onions
butter or margarine
salt and ground black pepper to taste
grated cheese, curry powder, chili powder, dried thyme, dried rosemary, or any other herb or spice desired (optional)

1. Onions may be baked in their skins. Wipe them, without peeling, and place them in a baking pan.
2. Bake in a hot oven until onions are tender.
3. Remove the onions from the oven, and peel off skins.

4. Serve hot with butter or margarine and salt and black pepper to taste.

5. If desired, sprinkle with grated cheese, curry powder, chili powder, dried thyme, or any other herb or spice desired.

Oven temperature: 425°F. (hot).

Baking time: 35 to 40 minutes.

Yield: 4 servings.

BRAISED GREEN PEPPERS AND ONIONS

6 medium-sized green peppers, seeded and cut into slices 1/4 inch thick

2 medium-sized raw onions, peeled and sliced 1/4 inch thick

1/2 cup sliced celery

3 tablespoons butter or margarine

1/4 cup snipped parsley or 1 tablespoon parsley flakes

1/4 cup beef broth or chicken broth

1 teaspoon salt or salt to taste

1/8 teaspoon ground black pepper

1. Prepare vegetables and set them aside.
2. Melt butter or margarine in a 9-inch skillet.
3. Add green peppers, onions, celery, and parsley. Cook, covered, 5 minutes, stirring occasionally.
4. Add beef or chicken broth, salt, and black pepper.
5. Cover and cook over low heat 10 to 15 minutes or until vegetables are tender. Serve promptly.

Yield: 6 servings.

BAKED POTATOES ON THE HALF SHELL

Baked potatoes served plain or fancy are always good eating. Prepare them with just a sprinkling of salt and pepper, and a little butter, or vary them with a tasty stuffing.

3 large white baking potatoes

3 tablespoons butter or margarine

1/4 cup milk

1 teaspoon salt or salt to taste

1/4 teaspoon ground black pepper

melted butter or margarine

1. Wash and dry potatoes and arrange them in a baking pan or on the oven rack.
2. Bake potatoes in a preheated very hot oven until they are tender when tested with a fork.
3. Cut potatoes in half lengthwise. Scoop out the insides, leaving shells intact so they can be refilled.
4. Mash potatoes with the next 4 ingredients until they are free from lumps.
5. Pile potato mixture into the potato shells, rounding them slightly. Brush tops with melted butter.
6. Arrange potatoes in a shallow baking pan, and brown them in the broiler oven. Or if desired, brown potatoes in a very hot oven.

Oven temperature: 450°F. (very hot).

Baking time: 45 to 60 minutes, depending upon size of potatoes. (If the oven is set for a dish at a lower temperature, bake potatoes along with it until they are tender. The baking time depends upon the temperature at which the oven is set.)

Yield: 6 servings (allow 1/2 large potato per serving).

VARIATIONS

POTATOES ON THE HALF SHELL WITH CHEESE

To the recipe for Potatoes on the Half Shell, add, after mashing, 1/2 cup shredded sharp American cheese. Mix well and continue according to directions.

POTATOES ON THE HALF SHELL WITH BACON

To the recipe for Potatoes on the Half Shell, add, after mashing, 6 slices crumbled, crisp bacon. Mix well and continue according to directions.

POTATOES ON THE HALF SHELL WITH DEVILED HAM

To the recipe for Potatoes on the Half Shell, add, after mashing, one can (6 ounces) deviled ham. Mix well and continue according to directions.

POTATOES ON THE HALF SHELL WITH MEAT OR FISH

To the recipe for Potatoes on the Half Shell, add, after mashing, 1 cup finely diced cooked roast beef, ham, lamb, or tongue, or a 6-1/2-ounce can well-drained tuna fish or crab meat. Mix well and continue according to directions.

BAKED SLICED POTATOES AND BACON

5 strips uncooked bacon

5 cups paper-thin slices potatoes

1-1/4 teaspoons salt

1/8 teaspoon ground black
pepper

1. Dice 2 strips of the bacon into a skillet and cook until bacon is about half done.
2. Drain off bacon drippings. Reserve, if desired.
3. Arrange alternate layers of sliced potatoes, sprinkled with salt and black pepper, and partly cooked bacon in a 1-quart casserole, rounding the potatoes over the top.
4. Cut remaining 3 strips of bacon in half, and arrange them over the potatoes.
5. Bake in a preheated hot oven until potatoes are tender and bacon is crisp.

Oven temperature: 400°F. (hot).

Baking time: Approximately 1 hour.

Yield: 6 servings.

BROWNED NEW POTATOES

24 (about 3 pounds) small new
potatoes

3/4 teaspoon salt

boiling water

6 tablespoons butter or margarine, melted

ground black pepper to taste

1. Thoroughly wash potatoes, but do not peel.
2. Put potatoes and salt in a 2-quart saucepan.

3. Pour in boiling water to a depth of 1 inch.
4. Cook, covered, until potatoes are tender when tested with a fork, but still retain their shape, 15 to 20 minutes.
5. Remove potatoes from saucepan, and dip them in melted butter or margarine.
6. Place potatoes in a shallow baking pan. Pour all the melted butter that is left over the potatoes, and sprinkle with black pepper to taste.
7. Bake in a preheated hot oven until potatoes have browned and skins are crisp, about 25 minutes.

Oven temperature: 400°F. (hot).

Baking time: 25 minutes.

Yield: 6 servings.

PARMESAN POTATOES

3/4 cup diced green pepper
3/4 teaspoon salt
2/3 cup milk .
_____
2 cups cubed, cooked potatoes
1/8 teaspoon ground black pepper

2 tablespoons butter or margarine
3 tablespoons grated Parmesan cheese

1. Put the first 3 ingredients in a 1-quart saucepan.
2. Simmer, covered, 5 minutes.
3. Add potatoes, black pepper, and butter, mix lightly, and turn mixture into a buttered 9-inch pie plate.
4. Sprinkle grated Parmesan cheese over the top.

5. Bake in a preheated moderate oven until cheese begins to brown.

Oven temperature: 350°F. (moderate).

Baking time: 15 minutes.

Yield: 4 servings.

TOPSY-TURVY POTATOES

5 medium-sized raw potatoes, peeled

3 small raw onions, peeled

1/2 medium-sized raw green pepper, seeded and stem removed

2 eggs, beaten lightly

1 teaspoon salt or salt to taste

1/8 teaspoon ground black pepper

3 tablespoons bacon drippings, butter, or margarine

1. Put potatoes, onions, and green peppers through a food chopper, using the medium blade, or chop very fine with a knife or vegetable chopper.
2. Mix chopped vegetables with the next 3 ingredients.
3. Heat bacon drippings, butter, or margarine in a 10-inch skillet. Add vegetable mixture, and spread it uniformly over the bottom of the skillet.
4. Cover and cook over low heat, without stirring, until vegetables have browned on the bottom and cooked through, 20 to 25 minutes.
5. Cut into wedges and serve with the browned side up.
   Yield: 6 servings.

BRANDIED SWEET POTATOES

A delicious dish for holiday meals or to serve to special guests any time of the year. The brandy may be replaced with 1/4 cup light cream.

4 cups hot mashed sweet potatoes (about 3-1/2 pounds raw sweet potatoes) or 2 cans (1 pound 2 ounce each) vacuum-packed sweet potatoes, drained

3 tablespoons sugar

4 tablespoons (1/2 stick) butter or margarine

1/2 teaspoon salt

1/4 cup apricot brandy or peach brandy

1 tablespoon grated orange rind

8 regular-size marshmallows

1. Put the first 5 ingredients in a 2-quart mixing bowl and mix well.
2. Turn mixture into a well-buttered 2-quart casserole, sprinkle with orange rind, and top with marshmallows.
3. Bake in a preheated moderate oven until the marshmallows have melted and browned. Serve hot.

Oven temperature: 350°F. (moderate).

Baking time: 25 to 30 minutes.

Yield: 6 to 8 servings.

SWEET POTATOES WITH BACON ON APPLE RINGS

A delicious accompaniment for ham, pork, or poultry. Allow 1 sweet potato and 1 apple ring per serving.

unpeeled apple rings, cut 1/2 inch thick, cores removed

whole, boiled, medium-sized sweet potatoes, peeled

uncooked bacon slices

orange juice or pineapple juice

1. Arrange apple rings on a generously buttered baking sheet.
2. Wrap each sweet potato with a slice of uncooked bacon. Hold ends in place with toothpicks. Place one sweet potato on each apple ring.
3. Pour 1 tablespoon orange juice or pineapple juice over each sweet potato.
4. Bake in a preheated hot oven until potatoes are hot and bacon is crisp.

Oven temperature: 400°F. (hot).

Baking time: 15 to 20 minutes.

BAKED ACORN SQUASH

Allow 1/2 medium-sized acorn squash for each serving. Wash the squash, cut in half lengthwise, and scrape out seeds and stringy portion. Stick a whole clove in each end of the squash halves, and put into each squash cavity the following ingredients:

1/16 teaspoon salt

1/16 teaspoon ground cinnamon

dash of ground black pepper

2 teaspoons dark or light brown sugar

1-1/2 teaspoons butter or margarine

1. Arrange squash in a baking pan. Pour boiling water into the pan to a depth of 1 inch.
2. Bake, covered, in a preheated hot oven (400°F.) 45 minutes.
3. Remove cover, and cook 15 minutes or until squash is tender.

STEAMED ACORN SQUASH

This is my favorite method of cooking acorn squash when only 3 to 4 servings are desired.

1. Place squash halves in a large saucepan or Dutch oven. (The saucepan should be between 3 and 4 inches deep).
2. Pour 1-1/2 inches boiling water into the pan.
3. Cover squash with foil to prevent water which condenses on the pan lid from dropping on the squash. Then cover pan with a tight-fitting lid.
4. Steam over medium heat 20 minutes or until squash is tender.

GRILLED TOMATOES

3 large tomatoes, washed and cut into crosswise halves

1 tablespoon lemon juice
1 teaspoon salt
1/2 teaspoon dried basil leaves or 1-1/2 teaspoons chopped fresh basil leaves (optional)

1/8 teaspoon ground black pepper

3 teaspoons butter or margarine
1 cup soft breadcrumbs
4 tablespoons (1/2 stick) butter or margarine, melted

1. Arrange tomato halves in a 9 x 9 x 2-inch baking pan, cut side up.
2. Combine the next 4 ingredients and sprinkle mixture over the tomato halves.
3. Dot each half with 1/2 teaspoon butter or margarine.
4. Blend breadcrumbs with melted butter or margarine and sprinkle them over the tomatoes.
5. Bake in a preheated broiler, 3 inches from source of heat, until the crumbs have browned, 4 to 5 minutes.

Broiler temperature: 500°F. (extremely hot).
Broiling time: 4 to 5 minutes.
Yield: 6 servings.

GLAZED TURNIPS

Plan to include these deliciously different turnips in your autumn and winter menus.

4 cups peeled, diced, raw turnips
1 cup boiling water
1 cup boiling beef stock or 1 beef bouillon cube and 1 cup boiling water

1/2 teaspoon salt
2 tablespoons sugar
2 tablespoons butter or margarine
dash ground mace or ground nutmeg

1. Put turnips and the 1 cup boiling water in a 2-cup saucepan. Cook, covered, 5 minutes.
2. Drain off water from turnips, add beef stock or beef bouillon cube and boiling water, salt, and sugar.

3. Cook, covered, about 10 minutes or until turnips are tender but not mushy.
4. Uncover, add butter or margarine and mace or nutmeg.
5. Cook, uncovered, until turnips are glazed, about 5 minutes, lifting turnips from bottom of pan with a fork frequently to prevent scorching. Serve hot.

Yield: 6 servings.

ZUCCHINI AND GREEN PEPPERS, ITALIAN STYLE

1 pound young tender zucchini squash, cut into 2 x 1/2-inch strips

3 medium-sized green peppers, seeded and cut into 2 x 1/2-inch strips

1/4 cup olive oil or salad oil

1 cup diced raw tomatoes

1 teaspoon salt or salt to taste

1/8 teaspoon ground black pepper

1. Prepare zucchini and green peppers and set aside.
2. Heat oil in a 9- or 10-inch skillet.
3. Add zucchini and green peppers, and fry them in the hot oil until vegetables have browned lightly.
4. Add tomatoes and salt. Simmer, uncovered, 10 minutes.
5. Stir in black pepper and serve hot.

Yield: 6 servings.

LOW-CALORIE RECIPES

If your doctor has prescribed a diet low in calories or low in sugar, the recipes in this section will help make your menus more interesting and more attractive not only for you but also for the rest of the family.

SOUPS

TOMATO-BEEF BROTH

2 cans (10-1/2 ounces each) beef broth

1 can (1 pint, 2 ounces) tomato juice

1/2 cup diced celery

1/4 cup shredded carrots

1 tablespoon instant minced onion

1/2 teaspoon salt or salt to taste

3/4 teaspoon dried oregano leaves (optional)

1/8 teaspoon ground black pepper

snipped parsley

1. Put all ingredients in a 2-quart saucepan and mix well.
2. Cook, covered, over low heat 15 minutes or until vegetables are tender and all flavors have blended.

293

3. Serve hot, sprinkled with snipped parsley.
Calories per serving: 64.
Yield: 4 cups or 4 servings, 1 cup each.

POTATO SOUP

The calories in this soup were reduced without reducing the flavor.

4 cups (1 pound) diced raw potatoes
1/2 cup chopped raw onion or 2 tablespoons instant minced onion
2 cups boiling water
1 teaspoon salt

2 cups skim milk
1/8 teaspoon ground black pepper
1 tablespoon bacon drippings
3 slices bacon, fried very crisp
snipped parsley or snipped chives

1. Put the first 4 ingredients in a Dutch oven or in a 3-quart saucepan. Cook, covered, until potatoes are very soft, about 25 minutes.
2. Remove Dutch oven or saucepan from heat and stir and mash potatoes until they are smooth.
3. Stir in milk, black pepper, and bacon drippings.
4. Heat until hot. Serve in soup bowls with 1/2 slice crisp bacon crumbled over each serving.
5. Garnish with snipped parsley or chives.
Calories per serving: 128.
Yield: 6 servings.

MUSHROOM SOUP

1/3 cup finely chopped raw onion or 2 tablespoons instant minced onion

1 cup chopped fresh mushrooms or frozen mushrooms

1/2 teaspoon celery salt

2 chicken bouillon cubes

2 cups skim milk
_____

salt and ground black pepper to taste

paprika or snipped parsley

1. Put the first 5 ingredients in the top of a 1-1/2-quart double boiler and place over boiling water.
2. Cook, covered, 20 minutes or until mushrooms are tender.
3. Add salt and black pepper to taste.
4. Serve hot garnished with paprika or snipped parsley.

Calories per serving: 56.

Yield: 4 servings.

MAIN DISHES

CHICKEN AND VEGETABLES CHINESE STYLE

1 cup thin, diagonal slices celery

1 cup sliced mushrooms (stems and caps)

2 cups slivered, cold, cooked chicken or turkey

1 tablespoon soy sauce

1 cup chicken broth or turkey broth
_____

2 teaspoons cornstarch

salt to taste

1/16 teaspoon ground black pepper

1 cup shredded head lettuce

1. Put the first 4 ingredients and 3/4 cup of the chicken or turkey broth in an 8- or 9-inch skillet.
2. Cook, covered, 4 to 5 minutes or only until the celery is crisp-tender.
3. Blend cornstarch with the remaining 1/4 cup chicken broth or turkey broth, add to the vegetables, and cook 1 to 2 minutes or until the liquid has thickened.
4. Season to taste with salt, if needed, and black pepper.
5. Fold in shredded lettuce just before serving.
6. Serve hot with cooked rice.

Calories per serving: 101.

Yield: 4 servings.

BAKED FISH PAPRIKASH

3 teaspoons butter or margarine (optional)

3/4 cup chopped raw onion or 2 tablespoons instant chopped onion softened in 2 tablespoons water

2 teaspoons imported paprika

4 servings (5 ounces each) fillet of haddock, halibut, perch, or flounder

3/4 teaspoon salt or salt to taste

1 teaspoon cornstarch

1/4 cup buttermilk

1. Rub 1 teaspoon of the butter, if used, over the bottom of a 10 x 6 x 2-inch baking dish.
2. Sprinkle onion and 1 teaspoon of the paprika over the butter or bottom of the dish.
3. Wipe fish with a damp cloth, and rub the salt over both sides of it.

4. Arrange fish over the onion and paprika and sprinkle it with the remaining 1 teaspoon paprika.
5. Dot fish with the remaining butter, if used.
6. Bake, covered, in a preheated moderate oven until fish flakes when tested with a fork.
7. Remove fish from oven. With a pancake turner transfer it to a warmed platter or serving plate.
8. Drain pan drippings into a small saucepan.
9. Blend cornstarch with buttermilk and add the mixture to the pan drippings. Mix well.
10. Stir and cook over surface heat to boiling point.
11. Serve sauce in a sauceboat to spoon over fish.

Calories per serving: 156 with butter; 126 without butter.
Oven temperature: 350°F. (moderate).
Baking time: 30 minutes.
Yield: 4 servings.

BROILED MACKEREL

1-1/2 pounds whole dressed mackerel
salt and ground black pepper to taste

2 teaspoons lemon juice
1/2 teaspoon dried tarragon leaves, crumbled
snipped parsley or paprika

1. Split mackerel lengthwise and cut it into 4 serving-size pieces.
2. Place the pieces, skin side down, in a foil-lined shallow baking pan.

3. Sprinkle with salt, black pepper, lemon juice, and tarragon leaves.
4. Broil in broiler oven with oven control set to broil until fish flakes when tested with a fork and is flecked with brown.
5. Serve hot garnished with snipped parsley or paprika.

Calories per serving: 170.

Broiler oven temperature: 550°F. (broil).

Broiling time: 8 to 10 minutes.

Yield: 4 servings.

SALADS

MOLDED APPLE CIDER SALAD

1 envelope unflavored gelatin
2 cups apple cider
dash salt
1 tablespoon lemon juice
_____
1/2 cup diced celery
1 cup shredded raw carrots

2 cups peeled and diced raw apples (about 3 medium-small apples)
_____
lettuce
cottage cheese (optional)

1. Soften gelatin in 1 cup of the cider.
2. Bring remaining 1 cup cider to boiling point and pour it over softened gelatin. Stir to dissolve gelatin.
3. Stir in salt and lemon juice.
4. Place bowl in a pan of ice water until mixture is as thick as fresh egg whites.
5. Fold in the next 3 ingredients.
6. Turn mixture into an 8 x 8 x 2-inch pan.

7. Chill until salad is firm and you are ready to serve it.
8. Cut salad into 9 squares and serve it on lettuce with about 1/4 cup cottage cheese, if desired.

Calories per serving: 62 without cottage cheese; 122 with cottage cheese.

Yield: 9 servings.

DEVILED EGG AND COTTAGE CHEESE SALAD

1/4 teaspoon pickle relish or 2 teaspoons finely chopped celery

1/2 teaspoon prepared mustard

1/2 teaspoon cider vinegar or tarragon vinegar

1/16 teaspoon instant minced onion

2 teaspoons milk
_____

2 hard-cooked eggs, peeled and cut into lengthwise halves

salt to taste

ground black pepper to taste

2 large lettuce leaves or 4 small lettuce leaves

4 tablespoons cottage cheese

1. Put the first 5 ingredients in a small mixing bowl.
2. Remove hard-cooked egg yolks from hard-cooked egg whites. Add yolks to seasoning mixture. Set whites aside.
3. Mash and stir the mixture until yolks are smooth.
4. Season to taste with salt and ground black pepper.
5. Spoon the mixture into the cavities of the hard-cooked egg whites.
6. Serve each 2 stuffed egg halves on 1 large lettuce leaf or 2 small lettuce leaves with 2 tablespoons cottage cheese.

Calories per serving: 109.

Yield: 2 servings.

CABBAGE AND CARROT SALAD

1-1/2 cups shredded green cabbage

1/2 cup shredded carrots

1/3 cup diced celery

1/2 teaspoon salt or salt to taste

ground black pepper to taste

1 teaspoon vinegar or lemon juice

2 tablespoons mayonnaise
_____

4 leaves lettuce

shredded carrots for garnish (optional)

1. Put the first 7 ingredients in a salad bowl and toss lightly, but well.
2. Serve on lettuce leaves.
3. Sprinkle with additional shredded carrots, if desired.

Calories per serving: 73.

Yield: 4 servings.

HERBED GREEN SALAD

2 tablespoons olive oil or salad oil

1 small clove garlic, cut in half, or 1/4 teaspoon instant minced garlic

10 large leaves romaine lettuce or 20 small inner leaves

10 large leaves curley endive or 20 small inner leaves

1/2 cup diced celery

1/2 cup diced green pepper
_____

1/2 teaspoon salt or salt to taste

1/2 teaspoon dried oregano leaves or 2 teaspoons chopped fresh oregano

1/8 teaspoon ground black pepper or pepper to taste

1 tablespoon lemon juice
_____

1 cup finely shredded raw carrots

1. Combine salad oil and garlic and let mixture stand 1 hour. If fresh garlic is used, remove it from the oil before adding oil to salad.
2. Meanwhile, wash salad greens, dry well, tear into bite-size pieces, and put in a large salad bowl.
3. Add celery, green pepper, and oil. Toss mixture lightly but thoroughly, being sure that each piece of the greens is coated with oil.
4. Sprinkle the next 4 ingredients over the top and toss lightly to prevent bruising the greens.
5. Garnish with shredded carrots. Serve promptly.

Calories per serving: 56.

Yield: 6 generous servings.

MOLDED PINEAPPLE-LIME SALAD

1 package (3 ounces) lime-flavored gelatin

1 cup hot water

1 cup crushed pineapple (8-1/4-ounce can), undrained

1/2 cup diced celery

1/4 cup sour cream

shredded lettuce

1. Dissolve gelatin in hot water in a 1-1/2-quart bowl.
2. Add pineapple and mix well.
3. Chill in the freezer or over ice water until the mixture begins to thicken, about 30 minutes.
4. Fold in celery and sour cream, mixing well.
5. Turn the mixture into a 3-cup mold or into an 8 x 8 x 2-inch pan.

6. Chill until gelatin is firm and ready to serve.
7. Cut salad into serving-size pieces, and serve on shredded lettuce.

Calories per serving: 92.

Yield: 6 servings.

GERMAN POTATO SALAD

1 pound potatoes (about 3 medium-sized)

2 slices lean bacon

1-1/2 tablespoons instant minced onion, or 1/3 cup chopped raw onion

1/2 teaspoon sugar

3/4 teaspoon salt or salt to taste

1/8 teaspoon ground black pepper

1/4 cup cider vinegar

1/3 cup beef broth, (bouillon cube, or canned broth or homemade broth)

1/2 cup diced celery

1. Wash potatoes and cook them, unpeeled, in boiling water to cover until they are tender but firm.
2. While potatoes are hot, drain and peel them and slice them into a 1-1/2-quart mixing bowl.
3. Fry bacon in a skillet until it is crisp. Remove bacon from skillet and drain on a paper towel. Pour bacon fat from skillet. (Discard it or save for other purposes.) Do not wash the skillet.
4. Put the remaining 7 ingredients in the unwashed skillet, bring mixture to boiling point, and pour it over the potatoes.

5. Break the bacon into bits and add to salad.
6. Toss lightly and serve hot.
Calories per serving: 119.
Yield: 4 servings.

TOSSED SHRIMP SALAD

4-1/2-ounce can shrimp, deveined

1 cup diced celery

2 cups coarsely shredded head lettuce

2 tablespoons mayonnaise

1 tablespoon French dressing, made with oil and vinegar

salt and ground black pepper to taste

snipped parsley

1 medium-sized unpeeled tomato, cut into 4 wedges

1. Put the first 3 ingredients in a large salad bowl.
2. Mix mayonnaise with French dressing and pour mixture over the salad. Sprinkle with salt and black pepper.
3. Toss salad lightly but well.
4. Garnish with snipped parsley and tomato wedges.
Calories per serving: 153.
Yield: 4 servings.

DESSERTS

ANISE COOKIES

2 cups sifted cake flour

1-1/2 teaspoons double-acting
  baking powder

1/2 cup (1 stick) butter or
  margarine, softened

1 teaspoon ground anise seed

1 teaspoon vanilla extract

5 teaspoons Sweet and Low
  sugar substitute

1/4 cup sugar

1 large egg

2 tablespoons water

1. Sift flour with baking powder and set aside.
2. Put the next 4 ingredients in a 1-1/2-quart mixing bowl and mix well.
3. Gradually blend in sugar. Beat in egg and water.
4. Stir in flour, 1/4 cup at a time. (This dough is stiff, but do not add more water or other liquid.)
5. Chill dough until it is stiff enough to handle — in the freezer 1 hour, in the refrigerator 2 to 3 hours.
6. Shape dough into 3/4-inch balls and place them 1-1/2 inches apart on ungreased cooky sheets.
7. Bake in a preheated moderate oven until cookies have browned around the edges.
8. Cool on wire racks. Store in airtight containers.

Oven temperature: 350°F. (moderate).

Baking time: 8 to 10 minutes.

Calories per cooky: 33.

Yield: 55 cookies.

MELON FRUIT CUP

1-1/2 cups diced fresh cantaloupe or honeydew melon
1-1/2 cups green seedless
grapes
1 cup orange sections

3 tablespoons lemon juice
2 tablespoons sugar or sugar
to taste, or sugar substitute
to taste
_____
sprigs fresh mint (optional)

1. Put the first 5 ingredients in a mixing bowl and mix lightly but well.
2. Chill at least 1 hour.
3. Serve in sherbet glasses or punch cups. Garnish with sprigs of fresh mint, if desired.

Calories per serving: 75 with sugar; 57 with sugar substitute.
Yield: 6 servings.

SUMMER FRUIT CUP

3 cups watermelon balls or
diced watermelon
1-1/2 cups pineapple wedges
(fresh or canned without
sugar)
1/4 cup sugar or sugar substitute to taste

3 tablespoons lime juice or
lemon juice
_____
1/2 cup blueberries
fresh mint leaves for garnish

1. Combine the first 4 ingredients and chill the mixture 1 hour or longer.
2. Add blueberries just before serving.

3. Serve in sherbet glasses, garnished with mint leaves.
Calories per serving: 68 with sugar; 43 with sugar substitute.
Yield: 8 servings.

COLD RASPBERRY SOUFFLÉ

1 envelope unflavored gelatin
1 teaspoon cornstarch
1 cup skim milk
12 drops Sweeta, or other liquid sugar substitute to equal 2 tablespoons sugar, or 2 tablespoons sugar

2 large eggs, separated
1 package (10 ounces) frozen raspberries, thawed
1/3 cup Cool Whip
1 teaspoon vanilla extract
1 teaspoon lemon juice

1. Combine gelatin and cornstarch in the top of 1-quart double boiler. Add milk and Sweeta or sugar and let the mixture stand 5 minutes.
2. Beat egg yolks lightly and add to gelatin mixture.
3. Cook, covered, over hot water (not boiling), stirring frequently, until mixture coats a metal spoon, 6 to 8 minutes.
4. Remove from heat and cool over ice water until custard begins to set. Meanwhile, put raspberries through a sieve. Stir sieved berries into the custard.
5. Fold in Cool Whip, vanilla extract, and lemon juice.
6. Beat egg whites until they stand in soft, stiff peaks and fold them into the mixture.
7. Turn soufflé mixture into a 1-quart soufflé dish. Chill until soufflé is spongy-firm and you are ready to serve it.
Calories per serving: 90 without sugar; 103 with sugar.
Yield: 6 generous servings.

COLD STRAWBERRY SOUFFLÉ

In the recipe for Cold Raspberry Soufflé, replace raspberries with 1 package (10 ounces) frozen sliced strawberries, thawed. Yield: 6 generous servings.

PINEAPPLE SPONGE

1 envelope unflavored gelatin
1/2 cup orange juice (fresh or frozen)
1 cup (8-1/4-ounce can) crushed pineapple
1 teaspoon lemon juice

1/2 teaspoon vanilla extract
1/4 cup Cool Whip
dash salt
2 large egg whites
1 tablespoon sugar

1. Mix gelatin with orange juice in a 1-1/2-quart mixing bowl. Let stand 5 minutes or until gelatin softens.
2. Place bowl in a pan of hot water to melt gelatin.
3. Stir in the next 3 ingredients.
4. Chill the mixture in a pan of ice water or in the freezer until it begins to thicken.
5. Fold in Cool Whip.
6. Add salt to egg whites, and beat them until they stand in soft, stiff peaks. Then beat in sugar.
7. Fold beaten egg whites into the pineapple mixture.
8. Spoon Pineapple Sponge into 6 sherbet glasses and refrigerate until you are ready to serve them.

Calories per serving: 71.
Yield: 6 servings.

TROPICAL BANANA MILK SHAKE

1 medium-sized ripe banana, sliced

2 tablespoons sugar or 12 drops Sweeta

2 teaspoons instant coffee

1-1/2 teaspoons vanilla extract

3 cups skim milk

1. Put all ingredients in a 2-quart mixing bowl and beat the mixture with a rotary beater or electric beater. Or if desired, put the first 4 ingredients and 1 cup of the milk in the jar of an electric blender, and blend mixture about 1/2 minute or until smooth. Stir in the remaining 2 cups milk.
2. Serve cold in tall glasses.

Calories per serving: 114 with sugar; 89 with Sweeta.

Yield: 4 servings.

LOW-SALT RECIPES

Some conditions require diets low in sodium. Although we obtain most of our sodium from sodium chloride (common table salt), sodium is also present in other foods. Since sodium is an essential nutrient, diets restricted in this element should be undertaken with a doctor's supervision. The following list of foods relatively low in sodium will be helpful in planning meals for such diets.

CEREALS: Buckwheat, farina, oatmeal, wheat cereals (unless sodium has been added during the processing; read the label for this information), macaroni, noodles, and spaghetti.

COFFEE AND TEA: Unless made with water high in sodium.

FRUIT AND FRUIT JUICES (canned and fresh): Pared apples, apricots, bananas, all berries, figs, grapes, grapefruit, oranges, peaches, pears, pineapple, and all fruit juices.

EGGS: Yolks only.

FATS: Unsalted butter, unsalted margarine, vegetable oils, and shortening.

MEATS: Foods from animal sources contain more sodium than do foods from plant sources. To provide adequate protein, one serving a day of one of the following is usually allowed: fresh or frozen beef, lamb, pork, veal, chicken, turkey, fresh fish (preferably freshwater fish).

MILK: Not over one glass daily since milk contains sodium.

VEGETABLES: Most fresh and frozen vegetables. Exceptions are: beets and beet greens, carrots, celery, chard, kale, spinach, and dandelion greens. Canned vegetables ordinarily have salt added during the canning process.

HERBS AND SPICES (These can be used to make food without salt more palatable.): basil, bay leaf, caraway seed, cinnamon, curry powder, dill weed, dill seed, garlic, ginger, marjoram, powdered mustard, nutmeg, mace, onion, rosemary, sage, savory, tarragon, and pepper. White pepper contains less sodium than black pepper. It is important to remember when buying or preparing baked products that baking soda and baking powder also contain sodium.

COLD BLUEBERRY-ORANGE SOUP

Family and guests will like this cold soup.

1 envelope unflavored gelatin
1/4 cup cold water
4 cups orange juice
3 tablespoons lemon juice

1/4 cup sugar
1-1/2 cups raw blueberries, washed and drained
sprigs of fresh mint (optional)

1. Soften gelatin in cold water and place it in a pan of hot water (not boiling) to melt.
2. Combine melted gelatin and the next 3 ingredients.
3. Refrigerate until mixture begins to thicken.
4. Fold in blueberries and chill mixture until you are ready to serve it.
5. Serve in bouillon cups or punch cups as the first course. Garnish with fresh mint if desired.

Yield: 8 servings.

BAKED CHICKEN BREAST IN ORANGE SAUCE

1/4 teaspoon cornstarch
2 teaspoons salad oil or un-salted butter or unsalted margarine, melted
2 tablespoons orange juice
1 teaspoon lemon juice

dash instant minced garlic
dash ground ginger
very small dash ground cin-namon
1 medium-sized chicken breast

1. Blend cornstarch with salad oil, butter, or margarine in a saucepan. Add the next 5 ingredients, mix well, and bring to boiling point.
2. Brush sauce over all sides of the chicken breast. Place it in a foil-lined shallow baking pan, skin side down.
3. Bake in a preheated hot oven 30 minutes, basting chicken once with the sauce.
4. Turn chicken, baste with sauce; and bake 10 to 15 minutes longer or until chicken is tender. Serve promptly.

Oven temperature: 400°F. (hot).

Baking time: 40 to 45 minutes.

Yield: 1 serving.

HERBED BROILED CHICKEN

1 tablespoon lemon juice
1 tablespoon salad oil or un-salted butter or unsalted margarine, melted

1/4 teaspoon of any of the following herbs:
crumbled dried basil leaves, crushed coriander seed, crushed dill seed, crumbled dried savory, crumbled dried tarragon, or dried sage
1 medium-sized chicken breast

1. Mix lemon juice and salad oil, butter, or margarine with any one of the herbs listed. Set aside.
2. Break the wing joint of the chicken breast so it will lie flat, and cut off and discard the wing tip.
3. Brush chicken breast on both sides with herbed lemon and

oil mixture and place, skin side down, on a rack in a foil-lined shallow baking pan.

4. Put chicken in a preheated broiler oven, with highest part of chicken 4 to 5 inches from source of heat.
5. Turn chicken as it browns, basting with the herbed lemon and oil mixture and pan drippings.
6. Cook until chicken is well done, 35 to 40 minutes.

Broiler temperature: 450°F. (very hot).

Broiling time: 35 to 40 minutes.

Yield: 1 serving.

BROILED HERBED LAMB CHOP

2 teaspoons salad oil
1 teaspoon lemon juice
1/16 teaspoon crumbled dried herb (basil, oregano, poultry seasoning, rosemary, sage, or tarragon)

dash ground white pepper
dash ground ginger

1 loin lamb chop, cut 3/4 to 1 inch thick

1. Combine the first 5 ingredients. Rub mixture on both sides of lamb chop. Reserve leftover oil mixture.
2. Place chop on a rack in a foil-lined shallow baking pan.
3. Broil in a preheated broiler oven until chop has cooked as desired, basting once with reserved herbed oil mixture.
4. Serve promptly.

Broiler oven temperature: 550°F. (broil).

Broiling time: 10 to 15 minutes.

Yield: 1 serving.

CURRIED BROILED HAMBURGERS

1 teaspoon lemon juice
2 teaspoons salad oil
1/16 teaspoon curry powder

dash powdered mustard

1/4 pound (1/2 cup) ground round steak

1. Combine the first 4 ingredients.
2. Shape ground meat into a patty 1/2 inch thick and brush both sides with the curry sauce.
3. Place patty in a foil-lined shallow baking pan.
4. Broil in a preheated very hot broiler oven until meat is cooked to desired doneness, basting with curry sauce 2 to 3 times. Serve promptly.

Broiler oven temperature: 550°F. (broil).
Broiling time: 8 to 10 minutes.
Yield: 1 serving.

POACHED SALMON
WITH SWEDISH LEMON SAUCE

1-1/2 cups boiling water
2 teaspoons white vinegar
1 teaspoon dill seed
1/4 small bay leaf
1 small onion, peeled and sliced

1 fresh salmon steak, about 3-1/2 to 4 ounces

Swedish Lemon Sauce (see following recipe)

1. Put the first 5 ingredients in a 1-quart saucepan and bring mixture to boiling point.

2. Put salmon steak in the boiling mixture, reduce heat, and simmer until fish flakes when tested with a fork, 8 to 10 minutes.
3. Using a pancake turner, transfer salmon to a serving plate, draining it well. Reserve fish stock.
4. Serve with Swedish Lemon Sauce.

SWEDISH LEMON SAUCE

2 teaspoons flour
1 tablespoon salad oil or un-salted butter or unsalted margarine, melted
1/3 cup fish stock (water in which fish was poached)

1 tablespoon heavy cream
2 teaspoons lemon juice
ground white pepper to taste
1/2 teaspoon snipped parsley

1. Blend flour with salad oil, melted butter, or margarine.
2. Add fish stock and cook, stirring frequently, until the mixture has thickened, 1 to 2 minutes.
3. Add cream and heat 1/2 minute.
4. Stir in lemon juice, pepper, and parsley. Serve over Poached Salmon.

Yield: 1 serving.

HERBED BROILED PERCH FILLETS

2 teaspoons salad oil, or un-salted butter or unsalted margarine, melted

2 teaspoons fresh lemon juice

1/4 teaspoon dried tarragon leaves or rosemary leaves, crumbled

very small dash ground ginger

very small dash instant minced garlic

1/4 pound perch fillets or other fresh-water fillets

1. Combine the first 5 ingredients.
2. Brush mixture over both sides of fish.
3. Place fish in a foil-lined shallow baking pan.
4. Broil in broiler oven with control set to broil until fish flakes when tested with a fork, brushing with the herbed sauce 2 to 3 times. Serve promptly.

Broiler oven temperature: 550°F. (broil).

Broiling time: 8 to 10 minutes.

Yield: 1 serving.

GREEN BEANS WITH CHIVES

1/2 cup cooked fresh or frozen green beans (without salt)

2 teaspoons unsalted butter or unsalted margarine

2 teaspoons lemon juice

1/2 teaspoon chopped chives

1. Combine all ingredients and heat only until hot.
2. Serve promptly.

Yield: 1 serving.

LIMA BEANS WITH CHIVES

In the recipe for Green Beans with Chives, replace cooked green beans with 1/2 cup cooked fresh or frozen lima beans, without salt. Continue according to directions in the recipe. Yield: 1 serving.

PANNED ZUCCHINI SQUASH

1 tablespoon unsalted butter or unsalted margarine

3/4 cup thin slices zucchini squash

1 small white onion, sliced thin

1/16 to 1/8 teaspoon dried basil leaves

ground white pepper to taste

1. Put the first 4 ingredients in a 1-quart saucepan.
2. Cover pan tightly to hold in the steam. Cook 5 to 7 minutes or until only crisp-tender over very low heat, stirring 1 or 2 times.
3. Add ground white pepper to taste. Serve hot.

Yield: 1 serving.

PANNED CABBAGE

1 tablespoon unsalted butter or unsalted margarine

1/16 teaspoon dill seed

1 cup finely shredded cabbage

ground white pepper to taste

1/4 teaspoon lemon juice

1. Melt butter or margarine in a 1-quart saucepan.
2. Add dill seed and cabbage.

3. Cover the pan tightly to hold in the steam. Cook 5 to 7 minutes over low heat, stirring 1 or 2 times.

4. Add ground white pepper to taste and lemon juice.

Yield: 1 serving.

FRUIT COMBINATIONS FOR DESSERTS

With the variety of fruits now available throughout the year, desserts should be no problem to anyone on a low-salt diet. The following combinations are suggested:

Blueberries and green seedless grapes with orange juice and sugar to taste.

Blueberries and pineapple wedges (fresh or canned) with lemon juice and sugar to taste. Refrigerate the mixture 1 to 2 hours before serving.

Green seedless grapes, sliced peaches, and diced pears (fresh or canned) with lemon juice or lime juice and sugar to taste. Refrigerate the mixture 1 to 2 hours before serving.

Green seedless grapes, sliced strawberries, and sugar to taste. Refrigerate 30 minutes before serving.

Green seedless grapes, sliced oranges, sliced grapefruit, and sugar to taste.

Grapefruit sections, orange sections, and sugar to taste.

Grapefruit sections, sliced strawberries, and sugar to taste.

Grapefruit sections, sliced peaches (fresh or canned), raspberries, and sugar to taste.

Orange sections and diced pears with lemon juice and sugar to taste.

Orange sections, sliced strawberries, and sugar to taste.

Orange sections, pineapple wedges (fresh or canned), sliced strawberries, and sugar to taste.

Sliced peaches and raspberries with lemon juice and sugar to taste.

Sliced peaches, green seedless grapes, and blueberries with lemon juice and sugar to taste. Refrigerate 1 to 2 hours before serving.

Sliced peaches, orange sections, and pineapple wedges (fresh or canned) with sugar to taste.

Sliced strawberries and fresh pineapple wedges with lemon juice and sugar to taste.

Strawberries, sliced bananas, orange juice, and sugar to taste.

Sliced strawberries, blueberries, green seedless grapes, and sugar to taste. Refrigerate 1 to 2 hours before serving.

INDEX